FAITH

AND

FREEDOM

IN LATIN AMERICA

By Dr. Teo A. Babun

BG Universal Press
2023

REFERENCES & CREDITS

Includes bibliographical references and index.
ISBN 978-0-9765016-5-7

Edited by Javier Pena
Design of Freedom Angel is provided by Jacobo Perez, is also an
advocate for freedom of religion in Central America

DEDICATION

For my wife Mary (Maija)

For those who suffer persecution because they seek human rights, especially the freedoms of expression and of freedom of religion or belief.

For my ministry partners and collaborators:
Norberto Quesada, Marcos Antonio Ramos, Carlos Sebastian, Mario Felix Lleonart, and many others.

Preface

Throughout my three-decade tenure as the head of an international faith-based nonprofit organization, dedicated to advocating for religious freedom and human rights in Cuba and across Latin America, I have encountered remarkable champions in this field driven and defined by two essential elements. One element finds its roots in the Universal Declaration of Human Rights (UDHR), a meticulously crafted document adopted by the United Nations General Assembly in 1948. Article 18 of the UDHR states that "Everyone has the right to freedom of thought, conscience, and religion; this right includes freedom to change his religion or belief, and freedom, either alone or in community with others and in public or private, to manifest his religion or belief in teaching, practice, worship, and observance."

The other element draws inspiration from the Bible, resonating with profound verses that emphasize the importance of upholding justice and defending the oppressed. Notably, Proverbs 31:8-9 (NIV) urges, "Speak up for those who cannot speak for themselves, for the rights of all who are destitute. Speak up and judge fairly; defend the rights of the poor and needy," while Psalm 82:3-4 (ESV) declares, "Give justice to the weak and the fatherless; maintain the right of the afflicted and the destitute. Rescue the weak and the needy; deliver them from the hand of the wicked."

As I delved deeper into the motivations of these brave individuals, I discovered historical examples of similar unwavering commitment. From the courageous acts of Corrie and Betsie ten Boom in Holland, risking their lives to save Jews from the clutches of the Nazis, to the tireless efforts of the late South African Archbishop Desmond Tutu in fighting for racial justice and condemning the oppressive apartheid regime, numerous others shared the same divine calling. Their work often found resonance in biblical verses such as "Defend the rights of the poor and needy" (Psalm 31:9(b)) and "My times are in your hands;

deliver me from the hands of my enemies, from those who pursue me" (Psalm 31:15). These scriptures formed the foundation of their lives and served as their shield against adversities. Their unwavering commitment was deeply rooted in the Bible.

Inspired by their resolve, I became impassioned to employ my own abilities in advocating for their cause and standing alongside them in their battles against tyrants and dictators who trample upon their God-given, fundamental rights. I have gathered the articles and opinion pieces I wrote over the years, intending to share their stories and motivations. Moreover, I strongly believe that freedom of religion is not only a fundamental human right but also a gift from God. My love for my family extends to love for my city, Miami, and country, and since God is the giver of love, freedom of religion is an essential right bestowed by God. Thus, my commitment to advocating for religious freedom is intertwined with my desire to be faithful to God in all that I do.

My work and passion have led me to deeply study Cuba, Nicaragua, and Venezuela. Each of these countries, while distinct, shares a troubling trait: they systematically infringe upon religious freedoms. Their governments exert strict control over religious expressions, denying their citizens the fundamental rights of expression, assembly, and worship. They suppress faith-driven gatherings and manipulate laws against conversion, blasphemy, and apostasy, punishing those who challenge their religious mandates.

I was compelled to shed light on these oppressive practices and refused to merely be a silent observer while such injustices prevailed.

I invite you to embark with me on this journey exploring the nexus between secular human rights and biblical teachings, recognizing the profound impact they have in molding our world. My hope is that this exploration will ignite in you a flame of compassion that leads you to embrace the divine duty of defending the marginalized and oppressed.

Prologue

In the heart of Latin America, a struggle for freedom unfolds under the oppressive shadow of governmental control. Faith and Freedom in Latin America takes you on a riveting exploration of the covert and overt tactics employed by governments to stifle religious expression, curtail fundamental rights, and maintain an iron grip on power.

Within these pages, you will bear witness to the relentless monitoring, control, and suppression of faith-based gatherings, as religious activity is forcibly confined within narrow boundaries dictated by the state. The violations of religious freedom are exposed, painting a vivid portrait of a region where speaking, gathering, and worshiping freely is deemed a threat.

Faith and Freedom in Latin America offers a detailed exploration of the stark violations of religious freedom in Cuba, Nicaragua, and Venezuela. It uncovers the state's tactics of surveillance, control, and suppression that inhibit religious communities from expressing their beliefs, congregating, and worshipping freely. Through compelling narratives, the book sheds light on the intricate mechanisms that restrict religious practices within strict state-dictated boundaries. Beyond its informative scope, Faith and Freedom in Latin America serves as a rallying cry, encouraging contemplation and motivating efforts to secure a future where religious liberty flourishes.

Yet, even in these trying times, glimpses of hope shine through. The book highlights the remarkable stories of intrepid individuals who bravely challenge these oppressive measures. These valiant religious leaders and devotees become the beacon of change, working ardently to pave the way for an era marked by peace, prosperity, and safety for their communities.

Furthermore, Faith and Freedom in Latin America champions the cause of faith-based activism in the quest for freedom and justice. It recognizes the nuanced history of the interplay between religion and politics, a topic that has stirred debates and divergent viewpoints throughout the ages.

Contents

Contents

FAITH
AND
FREEDOM
IN LATIN AMERICA

Introduction

"Resistance to tyrants is obedience to God."

Thomas Jefferson

Psalm 149:5-9 The Message
"Let true lovers break out in praise,

sing out from wherever they're sitting,
Shout the high praises of God,
brandish their swords in the wild sword-dance—
A portent of vengeance on the God-defying nations,
a signal that punishment's coming,
Their kings chained and hauled off to jail,
their leaders behind bars for good,
The judgment on them carried out to the letter
—and all who love God in the seat of honor!
Hallelujah!"

A relentless struggle for freedom of religion and belief unfolds silently across the globe. At its forefront stand valiant advocates who risk everything, even their lives, to safeguard this fundamental right for all citizens. Freedom of religion is far-reaching; it extends to thought, conscience, expression, assembly, and association, epitomizing the essence of individual choice and conviction. Recognized by international law and treaties, religious freedom underpins a peaceful, prosperous, and stable world, contributing to the foundations of secure societies. When people's beliefs are respected, they are empowered to achieve their full potential, uplifting entire communities in the process.

"Faith and Freedom in Latin America" aims to shed light on areas where the freedom of religion or belief is under siege. Governments across Latin America target religious minorities through various brutal tactics such as torture, unlawful surveillance, and detention in so-called re-education camps. Furthermore, they perpetrate faith-based discrimination, excluding religious minorities from specific professions or forcing them to work during their sacred observances. This book brings forth the untold narratives of these dauntless advocates, whose defiance and courage bear testament to the indomitable human spirit. Their struggle showcases the resilience and fortitude of those who refuse to yield to oppressive regimes seeking to suppress religious freedom.

Our exploration delves into the stories of those who have endured tremendous hardships for their staunch faith in nations like Cuba and Nicaragua. Here, governments weaponize laws against conversion, blasphemy, and apostasy—punishing those who defy their religious interpretations. These laws are deployed against humanists, atheists, and LGBTQI+ individuals, perpetuating discrimination and harassment against members of minority religious groups or those who resist conforming to officially sanctioned theology.

In the Latin American and Caribbean region, Cuba, Nicaragua, and Venezuela stand out as the primary violators of religious freedom. These nations wield tight control over religious activities, routinely denying citizens their basic rights to expression, assembly, and worship, including the suppression of faith-based gatherings. However, in these very countries, brave advocates for religious freedom persist. These are the individuals who choose to step up, halt the violations and abuses, and become part of the necessary change for their people to live in peace, prosperity, and security. This book is a tribute to their courage.

Religious freedom, as defined in Article 18 of the International Covenant on Civil and Political Rights, includes the rights to adopt, change, practice, and teach one's beliefs and gather in communities for worship and observance without coercion. Yet, violations of this freedom occur in many forms, with governments often employing deceptive tactics to mask their true intent.

For instance, in Nicaragua, the government manipulates the customs department to delay clearance of food cargo containers, effectively denying Catholic charities access to their donations. This action has a domino effect, leading to the charity discouraging donors from sending containers to avoid incurring heavy penalties, consequently depriving vulnerable Nicaraguans of food. Despite such challenges, brave advocates and civil society organizations continue to stand up against these violations, often at great personal risk.

This book also discusses the complex historical relationship between Christianity and politics, from early disputes to modern ideological divisions between the Christian right and left. Christianity has variously been used to support different political ideologies and philosophies, leading to a wide array of interpretations regarding Christian participation in politics. The text explores biblical guidelines for civil disobedience, emphasizing the importance of resistance against governments compelling evil acts and the permissibility of working to change governments that allow such acts.

"Defenders of Freedom in Latin America" brings forth the inspiring stories of those who combat religious freedom violations in Cuba, Nicaragua, and Venezuela. These brave individuals face daily human rights abuses under tyrannical governments. They endure persecution, imprisonment, expulsion, and branding as terrorists, all for defending the basic right to practice their faith freely.

In the pages of this book, we not only explore the present struggles of these courageous advocates in Latin America but also draw inspiration from historical accounts worldwide. We trace the echoes of religious persecution across time, underscoring the enduring influence of defenders of religious freedom emerging in various contexts.

In a world where freedom to believe is often an overlooked privilege, these stories underline the crucial need to protect and nurture this basic human right. They are a testament to the unyielding spirit of those who refuse to be silenced, their steadfast commitment shining as a beacon of hope for oppressed populations globally.

Join us on a journey into the lives of these extraordinary defenders of religious freedom. Their tales echo a collective call for justice, empathy, and the unwavering belief in the transformative power of faith, even amidst the darkest of times.

Section I
The Worst Religious Freedom Violators in Latin America

Introduction

In Cuba, as in Nicaragua and Venezuela, whose populations suffer rule by predatory authoritarians, the downtrodden often find comfort and practical help through their faith. Despite the constant harassment by the regime's enforcers, millions of citizens regularly worship and receive spiritual guidance from their religious leaders. But the regimes' policy toward religious actors is one of repression and tight control.

Freedom of religion is a fundamental human right, essential for the wellbeing and harmony of societies. However, in many countries across Latin America, this freedom has been systematically violated, leading to grave consequences for religious minorities and communities. While several nations in the region have witnessed religious freedom violations, this section of the book will shed light on the three worst offenders: Cuba, Nicaragua, and Venezuela. These countries have demonstrated a cunning and manipulative approach to suppressing religious liberties, making them prominent violators in the Latin American context.

Cuba: Suppressing Religious Leaders and Practices

In Cuba, the violation of religious freedoms is deeply rooted in the Machiavellian strategy adopted by the communist government against religious leaders of any faith. The Cuban authorities have historically viewed religious leaders and organizations with suspicion, perceiving them as potential threats to their regime. As a result, religious leaders are subject to surveillance, intimidation, and, in some cases, imprisonment.

Churches and places of worship face severe restrictions, with the government maintaining strict control over religious activities. Religious institutions are required to register with the government, making them susceptible to interference and monitoring. This registration process often serves as a tool to suppress religious expression and propagate state ideologies.

Despite the challenges, religious communities in Cuba have shown remarkable resilience, finding ways to preserve their faith and cultural heritage even under oppressive circumstances. The Cuban people's devotion to their beliefs has served as a testament to the power of faith in the face of adversity.

Nicaragua: War Against the Catholic Church

In Nicaragua, the violation of religious freedoms have reached a peak under Ortega's rule, with the Catholic Church in particular becoming a target of aggression. Ortega declared war against the Catholic Church, leading to the expulsion of nuns and the representative of the Vatican. Additionally, Monsignor Rolando Alvarez, a prominent bishop, has been unjustly imprisoned for speaking out against the government's actions.

These measures were part of a broader campaign to weaken the Church's influence and align religious institutions with the state's ideology. Such actions not only violated the freedom of religion but also violated the principle of separation of church and state, compromising the autonomy and independence of religious organizations.

No wonder the pope, who normally refrains from caustic characterizations, said of Ortega: "I have no other choice but to think that the person in power is mentally unbalanced." In a March 2023 interview with an Argentine publication, Francis accused the Ortega regime of melding Leninism and Hitlerian fascism. It is a "crass dictatorship," he said.

The State Department describes conditions in Nicaragua as "an ongoing sociopolitical crisis [that] began in April 2018 when regime-controlled police violently crushed a peaceful student protest." Since those crackdowns, the government has gone on to kill at least 325 people, imprison hundreds, injure thousands and exile more than 100,000.

Despite the persecution, the Catholic Church in Nicaragua has continued to be a resilient defender of freedom and human rights, advocating for justice and peace in the face of adversity.

Venezuela: Desecrating Places of Worship

In Venezuela, religious freedom violations have escalated dramatically under the rule of Maduro. The government's actions have been particularly egregious, with instances of invading churches during Sunday Mass and disrupting religious gatherings. Such actions have created havoc and fear among religious communities, infringing upon their right to worship and practice their faith peacefully.

Furthermore, religious leaders who dare to speak out against the government's actions face retaliation, including arrest and imprisonment. The Venezuelan government's disregard for religious freedom demonstrates a blatant abuse of power, leading to the erosion of trust between the state and its citizens.

Conclusion

In conclusion, Cuba, Nicaragua, and Venezuela stand out as the three worst religious freedom violators in Latin America. The governments of these nations have demonstrated a troubling pattern of suppressing religious leaders, restricting places of worship, and silencing dissenting voices within religious communities.

It is essential for the international community to remain vigilant and hold these governments accountable for their violations of religious freedom. Protecting religious liberties is not only a matter of upholding human rights but also essential for fostering a society that values diversity, tolerance, and mutual respect. Only by confronting these violations and advocating for change can we work towards creating a Latin America where religious freedom is respected and protected for all.

Section II

The Suppression of Religious Liberties in Cuba

Introduction

A poignant insight into the suppression of religious freedoms in Cuba comes from Father Alberto Reyes, a Catholic Priest from Camaguey, Cuba. On December 14, 2022, Father Reyes voiced his concerns in a Facebook post titled "I've Been Thinking XV." His words powerfully encapsulate the distressing state of religious freedom in Cuba.

It reads as follows:

"I've been thinking about... religious liberty".

Those of us who are alive are always in tension. I say "alive" because there are those who are still around but have already decided to die: they do not think, they do not dream, they lack vision.

This "life in tension" starts from the present and is nourished by ideals and possible dreams. Thus, from the present, the desirable future is visualized, and we tend towards it.

But it is very important that the tension be just because it is one thing to tend towards a desirable future and another to alienate oneself, imagining oneself in a world that is desired but does not exist today.

I have many dreams that, from my present, exert tension toward my future: I dream of a country where there is political plurality, a healthy economy, freedom of expression, social discipline but not repression... and I dream of a country where there is religious freedom, which is not reduced to believers being able to gather in our temples to worship the God who gathers us.

> • If there were religious freedom in my country, there would not be an Office of Religious Affairs in charge of controlling the practice of the faith, of controlling every movement of the Church and of

calling the bishops and superiors when what a priest or religious says or does bothers them, to get them to "leash" the priest or religious person while those who give the orders keep their hands clean.

• If there were religious freedom in my country, churches would have access to the means of social communication, and we could offer our radio and television programs, to make known through them the Gospel of Jesus Christ, which we consider to be the best program of life that exists.

• If there were religious freedom in my country, churches would be able to participate in the educational system and play a role in the formation of new generations, introducing religious classes in for those who want them, or establishing their own schools that allow parents to choose the education they want for their children, according to their faith, beliefs, and values.

• If there were religious freedom in my country, churches would have access to the health system, being able to offer the population more health care alternatives.

• If there were religious freedom in my country, we would not have to depend on permits to publicly manifest our faith, and we could plan and organize public masses, processions, Stations of the Cross in the streets, Christmas parades... just by informing the authorities about our use of public spaces.

• If there were religious freedom in my land, the construction of temples would be allowed in those places where there are established Christian communities which, in the absence of a temple, have to meet in private homes.

• If there were religious freedom in my land, churches destroyed by hurricanes or damaged by the passage of time could be rebuilt by a simple reconstruction process and would not have to undergo a long process of authorizations that can last for years while the communities survive as best, they can.

• If there were religious freedom in my land, churches considered "illegal", which were built without the corresponding permits because those permits never arrived, would not be demolished.

• If there were religious freedom in my land, the official registration of new Christian denominations that want to exercise their right to evangelize in Cuba would be allowed.

• If there were religious freedom in my country, Christians who think differently from the official government discourse would not be prevented from participating in religious celebrations. Nor would lay people, the religious and priests who express opinions different from those of the government be continually harassed with chastisements and, of course, they would not be "regulated," preventing their mobility, nor would they be expelled from the land where they want to remain and serve.

• If there were religious freedom in my land, there would be no accusations or denigration of priests, religious men and women and lay people who, moved by their faith, raise their voices to denounce social injustices and seek to accompany those who are victims of those injustices, exercising their baptismal identity as prophets.

All this would be possible if there were religious freedom in my country... but there is none."

In his reflection, Father Reyes dreams of a nation where political plurality, a thriving economy, freedom of expression, and above all, religious freedom thrive. He envisions a future where the Church can fully participate in society - engaging in education, contributing to the health system, and freely organizing public masses and processions. He longs for a Cuba where Christian communities can construct temples without impediments and those damaged by natural or man-made disasters can be rebuilt without extensive authorization processes.

He yearns for a country where Christians who voice their dissent are not ostracized or penalized, where new Christian denominations can freely evangelize, and where religious organizations can exercise their right to spread their message through media outlets. Yet, as he concludes, such a Cuba does not currently exist.

Historical Background

Since the takeover by the Communist Party of Cuba in 1959, the government has imposed tight restrictions on the Church, often responding to dissent and criticism with strict penal measures. The government's control over religious institutions, from denying registration to new churches to the imposition of fines and confiscation of properties, has significantly curtailed the Church's influence.

The single-party rule of the Communist Party has led to a surveillance state where any critique of the government's authority is deemed a threat to the regime. The resulting repression and infringement of citizens' rights have forced Christians to compromise their beliefs to access basic services. The COVID-19 pandemic has further heightened the regime's stranglehold over its citizens, especially Christians who openly contradict the government's interests based on their faith.

In the face of rampant corruption and impunity, the government wields the state apparatus to maintain its power. Christians across denominations live under constant fear of reprisals for expressing their views or supporting anti-government protests.

Freedom of Religion in Cuba: A Mirage

Cuba, a single-party state under the Cuban Communist Party, regulates and controls religious institutions through the Office of Religious Affairs (ORA) of the Central Committee of the Cuban Communist Party. The Law of Associations necessitates that religious organizations register with the Ministry of Justice, which is home to the ORA. This office exercises arbitrary control over registered religious organizations, requiring permission for virtually any activity other than regular worship services.

Church in Cuba: A Historical Perspective

Christianity in Cuba was established in 1512 through Roman Catholic priests of the Dominican order as a consequence of Spanish colonization. Protestant activity can be traced back to 1741 during British occupation. The introduction of slaves from Africa in the 1800s led to the development of Santeria, a syncretistic cult that blends Roman Catholic faith with Yoruba customs.

After gaining independence from Spain in 1898, Cuba's dependency on the U.S. led to the establishment of many Protestant churches and movements, including Methodists, Adventists, Presbyterians, Quakers, Baptists, and Lutherans.

The Protestant community in Cuba is small but resilient. After a slump in the 1970s, the community experienced a resurgence, with growing numbers of followers and increased church activities. The Protestant movement in Cuba now accounts for roughly 4.8 percent of the total population.

The Current State of the Evangelical Church

The Evangelical Protestant church community in Cuba has diverse political views, primarily falling under three categories: "official," "semi-official," and "extra-official."

Despite their cooperation with the government, members of the Cuban Council of Churches (CCC) still experience divisions between denominations. The government often rewards compliant churches with benefits such as building permits, international donations, and exit visas for pastors.

However, governmental, cultural, and systematic barriers hinder religious freedom. Even though foreign support is permitted, bureaucratic obstacles and latent anti-Christian sentiments within the government present significant challenges. The government's refusal to codify church services and their constant accusations against faith-based institutions create an environment of fear and uncertainty.

The barriers to Christian expression are significant. Religious literature distribution outside church buildings is banned, as are Christian television and radio programs. Denominations are barred from operating schools, and there are strict regulations on how churches can organize, raise funds, evangelize, and proselytize. These constraints leave people uncertain about the boundaries of their religious expression.

Contextual Overview on Freedom of Religion and Belief in Cuba

Although the Cuban Constitution explicitly mentions religious liberty, these freedoms are circumscribed by the supremacy of socialism and communism, thereby granting the government considerable authority to control various societal aspects. Through numerous laws and past regulations that cover housing, intra-country mobility, building permits, registration requirements, exit permits, and activities for foreign visitors, the Cuban government maintains a stranglehold over its citizens.

Articles 8 and 55 of the Cuban Constitution acknowledge, respect, and guarantee religious liberty, a tenet that aligns with international standards on religious freedom. Nevertheless, these rights are later modified by Article 62, which prioritizes the socialist and communist state's preservation and objectives over fundamental human rights, including those concerning religious liberty.

The Cuban Penal Code (Chapter IV, Article 206), termed 'Abuse of Liberty of Worship,' further curtails the rights elaborated in Article 55. This provision allows the state to penalize a broad array of religious activities that may not endanger public order. However, Cuba does not participate in the Inter-American Convention on Human Rights that safeguards freedom of religion and conscience. Despite signing the International Covenant on Civil and Political Rights and the International Covenant on Economic, Social and Cultural Rights, Cuba has not ratified these agreements that also contain clauses to safeguard religious freedom.

In highlighting the transgressions against Freedom of Religion and Belief (FoRB) in Cuba, the following points elucidate the laws and regulations exploited by the Cuban government:

- Cuba's constitution and laws largely fail to align with international FoRB standards, with the country failing to meet 34 f 36 FoRB indicators developed by Dr. Ahmed Shaheed when he served as the UN's Special Rapporteur on Freedom of Religion or Belief."

- The new constitution, approved in April 2019, weakens FoRB safeguards compared to the prior constitution. While it retains much of the language from the 1976 constitution, it excludes the regulation of religious institutions by law. In a society where FoRB rights are recognized and respected, regulation of religion would not be necessary. But this is not the case in Cuba.

- Constitutionally established rights are unenforceable due to the lack of a constitutional court, an appeal procedure for judicial review of constitutional rights, and a Criminal Procedure Law that does not invoke or define how to enforce constitutional rights.

• The constitution is not compatible with internationally accepted standards as it yields to laws that can contradict constitutionally established rights. It lacks the power to reform laws when they are unconstitutional and defines the Communist Party as the "superior" state power without regulation in the constitution.

• Rights complementary to FoRB cannot be defended due to the absence of legal mechanisms or legislation to protect against religious discrimination, hostility, or violence.

• Cuba does not adhere to its constitution. The constitution and many other codes and laws serve as a showcase to bolster its socialist system and human rights guarantees to international organizations like the UN. However, the Cuban government governs without upholding the 2019 constitution approved by the National Assembly.

• The Communist Party, being a supra-Constitutional entity with no legal framework for religious rights, governs religious freedom in Cuba. Its Office of Religious Affairs (ORA), derived from and dependent on the Communist Party's Central Committee, works obscurely and without legislation.

• A reform of the Law on Associations is not imminent. The current law prohibits the registration of any association that is independent of the State, including religious organizations. Interviewed faith leaders believe a new law may be used to further regulate and limit FoRB rights. The lack of legal standing of faith organizations is a central issue.

• A significant majority of independent faith leaders assert they are actively repressed, with 52 out of the 56 surveyed reporting frequent experiences of threats, violence, detentions, and acts of repudiation.

• The ORA coordinates state repression of FoRB rights. Almost all interviewed faith leaders believe the ORA arbitrarily controls FoRB and employs State Security and other government entities to carry out discreditation campaigns and restrict FoRB rights.

• State-controlled proxy organizations pose as religious entities to dominate the representative space of real religious organizations and discourage interfaith unity.

• FoRB repression is tailored to each faith group. Although the Catholic church appears to have more operational independence due to the Vatican's power, it has experienced substantial repression since the revolution.

• The Cuban government employs comprehensive tactics and motives to repress FoRB. These include harassment, threats, physical attacks, confiscation of property, defamation, accusations of illegal or immoral behavior, denial of rights of employment or education, and use of the COVID-19 pandemic and currency unification as pretexts to limit FoRB rights.

• The government impedes faith community operations and social services, with 93% of faith leaders agreeing that the government prevents the social actions of churches.

• State education promotes atheism, despite the constitutional declaration that Cuba is a secular state. The majority of respondents believe education is based on atheist ideology, with students not permitted to dress according to their religious traditions.

The Office of Religious Affairs' Role in Religious Regulation

In Cuba, the Office of Religious Affairs (ORA), an arm of the Central Committee of the Cuban Communist Party, exercises authority over religious groups and associations. This unique arrangement requires these groups to seek authorization for any activity from the ORA, a non-governmental entity, without any available appeal process. The primary focus of the ORA is to regulate and restrict both public and private expressions of religious faith, rather than safeguard the religious freedom of the Cuban citizens.

Directed by Caridad del Rosario Diego Bello, a Central Committee member, the ORA exhibits a consistent pattern of antagonism towards religious groups. Decisions and permits are issued centrally from Havana, giving the ORA immense power over religious associations and their members due to its lack of a clear legal framework. Frequent refusal or non-response to requests, such as building or repair permits, is a common issue. The ORA also has a history of capriciously denying church leaders' requests for travel.

Government agencies, like the Ministry of Housing and the Ministry of Public Planning, often collaborate with the ORA to target religious groups. This complex interplay often leads to bureaucratic deadlocks, as in the case of the Second Baptist Church in Alamar, Havana. This church has been unable to register its building since 2009 due to both the Ministry of Public Planning and the ORA demanding the other grant approval first.

The Cuban Government's Suppression of Worship

Religious freedom violations documented by faith-based organizations working in Cuba primarily involve the government denying citizens the right to worship. In 2021 and the first quarter of 2022, thousands of these cases were reported, with many victims considered political dissidents by the government.

State security agents would often block individuals from attending Sunday services either by physically surrounding their homes or detaining them for the duration of religious services. This interference extended beyond Sunday services to other religious events, such as Bible studies and prayer groups.

These rights infringements primarily impacted Roman Catholics, but other denominations experienced similar incidents. For instance, two families reported persistent harassment as they tried to attend services at the Central Methodist Church in Holguín Province.

The Cuban government's attempt to control the public narrative around religious freedom was most apparent during Pope Benedict XVI's visit in March 2012. In an ironic bid to present an image of religious freedom, the government detained hundreds of practicing Catholics deemed political dissidents, thereby preventing their participation in any religious events during the Pope's visit.

Penalties for Non-Collaboration

The Cuban government has a long-standing strategy to enforce the social isolation of individuals it deems troublesome. Pressure is often exerted on pastors and priests to expel certain congregational members involved in independent journalism, human rights activism, or pro-democracy activism, viewed by the government as counter-revolutionary activities.

As defiance among religious groups grows, the government has increased surveillance and threats to close non-compliant churches. It also often approaches congregation members, pressuring them to file complaints against church leaders.

The government has also targeted churches that refuse to comply, such as the Trinidad Baptist Church in Santa Clara. Despite its pastor stepping down in 2010, the church's bank accounts remain frozen due to its refusal to bar certain individuals from attending church activities.

Family members of dissidents are regularly targeted as well. For instance, the mother of a well-known Havana-based dissident was barred from attending her longtime Baptist Church. Church leaders across Cuba also report being coerced into publicly supporting government and Cuban Communist Party initiatives, with those who refuse often becoming targets of harassment campaigns.

The Persistent Muzzle on Dissenting Voices

Cuban church leaders persistently report intense pressure from the government to suppress any critical voices within their religious circles. Those who failed to conform to official demands faced aggressive repercussions in the past year. Earlier, the government's concern seemed focused primarily on church leaders from the Cuban Council of Churches (CCC), which has played a pivotal role in portraying a global image of Cuba respecting religious freedom. However, since 2012, non-CCC denominations also reported immense pressure to silence or expel leaders who vocally critiqued the government and its policies.

One striking example is Reverend Mario Félix Lleonart Barroso, the pastor of the Taguayabon Ebenezer Baptist Church, who was also a teacher of theology at the Santa Clara seminary affiliated with the Western Baptist Convention. He first attracted the government's ire when he offered spiritual support to Guillermo Fariñas during his 2010 hunger strike. Reverend Lleonart Barroso established the blog "Cubano Confesante" with the support of renowned Cuban blogger Yoani Sánchez. In his blog, he openly condemned violations of religious freedom in Cuba. His pastoral duties, including providing spiritual support to local human rights activists and publicly denouncing the brutal death of a parishioner, Juan Wilfredo Soto, at the hands of the police, made him a prime target of the government. Following that, he was arbitrarily detained, openly stalked, and threatened by state security agents regularly.

After failed attempts to expel Reverend Lleonart Barroso by pressuring the Western Baptist Convention, the authorities resorted to coercion tactics, including threats of job loss, to manipulate members of the Ebenezer Baptist Church congregation into filing a complaint against the pastor. When this tactic bore no fruit, the denominational leadership was pressured to alter its leadership and decision-making structures, presumably making them more susceptible to government intervention. Today Reverend Barroso lives in exile in the Washington, D.C., area, where he continues to work for religious freedom in Cuba.

Government Surveillance in Churches

The widespread and persistent infiltration of government informants in churches and seminaries is another testament to the regime's systematic control. Since 1959, the government has planted spies in all religious congregations and institutions to monitor activities, including the content of sermons, and report anything deemed counter-revolutionary or critical of the authorities. This practice has instigated a form of self-censorship among church leaders, who are cautious not to utter anything potentially construed as anti-Castro or counter revolutionary.

This strategic surveillance is driven by the government's acute awareness of the potential role of religious groups in overthrowing repressive regimes. Consequently, religious leaders, being among the few non-Communist Party members permitted to address the public, are viewed as a potential threat. The deliberate employment of spies and informants results in a pervasive atmosphere of intimidation, severely impeding Cubans' right to worship freely.

Intimidation and Attacks on Church Leaders

A consensus among church leaders across denominations suggests that the government's focus on individual leaders has intensified, characterized by overt threats and intimidation tactics in recent years. These methods, often carried out covertly and verbally, make it difficult to document or report them. Typical threats involve consequences such as restricting educational opportunities for the target's children, loss of job, vehicle, or housing, or failure to cooperate with the authorities.

Increasingly, church leaders have reported frequent unscheduled visits from state security agents to their homes with the explicit aim to intimidate. Similarly, high-level officials often convene meetings with church leaders solely to remind them of the government's surveillance. Severe harassment, including violent acts, is typically reserved for church leaders who have publicly opposed the government or stood up for religious freedom.

Refusal to Register New or Independent Religious Groups

The government mandates that churches and other religious groups register with the provincial office of the Registry of Associations, under the Ministry of Justice. However, these entities also fall under the purview of the Office for Attention to Religious Affairs (ORA), directed by Caridad Diego. About 54 state-registered denominations or church groups exist, more than half of which are members of the CCC, historically favoring the government.

Restrictions on Movement Within Cuba

The government regularly refuses to acknowledge a change of residence for pastors and other church leaders assigned to new churches or parishes, making relocation a significant hurdle. Under Decree 217, signed by Fidel Castro in 1997, which imposed restrictions on internal migration, pastors and their families often find it challenging to register their new place of residence.

Refusal of Exit Visas and Government Permits

The government often denies individuals permission to travel abroad under perceived, albeit undefined, threats to national security.

House Churches

Faith-based organizations working in Cuba reported continuous transgressions concerning home-based churches known as "House Churches" (Casas Culto). The Cuban government has been persistently trying to push all denominations and churches to register their affiliated home-based churches over the last decade. Yet, these attempts are rarely executed uniformly.

Simultaneously, many churches that have tried to register encountered rejection or didn't receive any response to their application. The faith-based organizations working in Cuba estimate that the majority of home-based churches, the count of which is continually increasing, remain unregistered.

The majority of House Churches align with a historical, recognized denomination. However, the number of independent Housee Churches or those associated with unrecognized religious groups has grown. These groups, which did not exist before 1959, do not have registered buildings for religious use. Their entire physical infrastructure comprises home-based churches, making them an easy target for the government and particularly vulnerable due to their lack of recognized religious protection. For instance, a Latter-Day Saints (Mormon) Church in Havana was targeted in late 2012, with the government denying or ignoring all its attempts to register with the Office of Religious Affairs (ORA). The church was eventually shut down by agents from the Department (responsible for cultural affairs) of the Ministry of the Interior (MININT).

In 2010, Caridad del Rosario Diego Bello explicitly mentioned to CCC leaders in Havana that the ORA, presumably backed by the government, was planning to close all new religious groups, highlighting the Apostolic Movement and the Growing in Grace religious group. According to a recording of her speech shared with the faith-based organizations working in Cuba, this would be achieved by seizing and demolishing houses where religious activities were held. Even after three years, the policy remains unchanged.

Even religious congregations without physical buildings haven't escaped the government's assault. For instance, a large church in San José de las Lajas, Havana Province, affiliated with the Apostolic Movement and led by Pastor Tony Ortiz, has faced ongoing problems. Despite repeated attempts to register, their applications have been denied. Pastor Ortiz reported regular threats by local officials to seize the property if religious activity did not stop.

Faith-based organizations working in Cuba are concerned that Directive 43 and Resolution 46, both issued in April 2005, which imposed complex and repressive restrictions on House Churches, are in effect. They fear that the government may enforce this legislation on any church that attempts to register, potentially leading to the closure of a significant proportion of these churches.

The directive states that two home-based churches of the same denomination will not be allowed to exist within two kilometers of each other. It also requires detailed information, including worshipers' count, service dates and times, and the names and ages of all residents of the house in which services are held, to be provided to the authorities.

Upon granting authorization, the authorities are allowed to supervise the operation of meetings. The directive also explains that if the authorities find that the requirements for operating a House Churches are not being met, they can suspend meetings in the house for a year or more. Any complaint against a church could lead to its permanent shutdown and attendees may face imprisonment.

The legislation also explicitly bans non-Cubans from participating in a religious service, including simply being present, without official permission. Foreigners are entirely prohibited from associating with House Churches in mountainous regions. Any violation of this clause results in fines of approximately US$1,000, a huge amount for Cubans who earn less than US$20 per month on average. The fine is applied both to the foreigner involved and the church leader responsible, and the home-based church will be shut down.

Finally, even if a House Church is authorized to operate, it must adhere to the limits imposed by the authorities. Rooms within the house that have not been approved cannot be used by the home-based church, nor can the church members meet on the roof, a common practice in Cuba due to heat and space constraints.

Contextual Background of House Churches

During the 1990s, the rapid growth of all denominations and the shortage of spaces designated for religious activity led to the widespread use of House Churches. This term applies to structures that are either used as family homes for part of the week and for church services on specific days, or homes dedicated solely to religious activities. The term also includes buildings constructed without specific permission for religious use.

The size of individual home-based churches varies greatly. Some have only a few regular attendees, while others have congregations numbering in the hundreds. It's impossible to know the exact number of home-based churches in Cuba, but local church leaders estimate the number to be anywhere between 10,000 and 15,000.

Few House Churches have been granted formal authorization to carry out religious activities. In Cuba, where freedom of assembly and association are severely restricted, this carries obvious risks. Meetings of more than fifteen people are technically illegal. Some churches have attempted to circumvent this by establishing multiple House Churches and limiting the maximum number of attendees at each to fourteen. Others keep no written records of addresses and names of House Churches hosts and change their locations frequently.

Religious Discrimination in Cuba

Religious discrimination in Cuba has been reported consistently, mainly by Christians, who have experienced varying degrees of bias in workplaces and educational institutions. The level of discrimination varies across different regions, often correlated with the attitudes of local and regional authorities. Many church leaders do not think there is a central government policy actively promoting discrimination against Christians. However, they note that the government openly tolerates such prejudice, with employers and officials who discriminate against religious believers rarely facing repercussions for their actions.

A notable instance of sanctioned discrimination involved Alejandro Francisco Amador, an evangelical Christian from Old Havana. He reported that police and Committees for the Defense of the Revolution (CDR) officers visited his home, declaring the Bible verse (John 8:3210) he posted on his door as "dangerous" and "counter revolutionary." The Bible verse reads "Then you will know the truth, and the truth will set you free" (NIV). This visit occurred during routine checks on a police list, initially meant for monitoring criminals and the unemployed, but also included Protestant Christians. When questioned, the officials stated that they considered Christians "persons of interest for State Security."

Children seem especially vulnerable to religious discrimination. Authorities often use threats of limiting or even eliminating their prospects for further education as leverage. One alarming incident happened in March 2013, when a young girl from a Baptist church in Ciego de Avila Province was excluded from school and threatened with expulsion for refusing to announce that "Comandante Hugo Chávez (former President of Venezuela) was more important than Jesus Christ" during compulsory memorial activities following President Chávez's death.

Religious leaders agree that Seventh Day Adventists and Jehovah's Witnesses face unique challenges because of their refusal to participate in patriotic activities on the Sabbath. These students are frequently targeted for harassment and ridicule, often denied university admission, and some who get in are later suspended. The Adventists also encounter particular difficulties due to their refusal to work on Saturdays, a day they consider sacred.

A significant case of religious discrimination unfolded in August 2012 in Granma Province. A ten-year-old Jehovah's Witness student was demoted to third grade from fifth as punishment for her refusal to participate in a school 'prayer' exalting Che Guevara and the 'Cuban Five' (Cuban spies incarcerated in the U.S.). The girl had previously had conflicts with school officials over her refusal to sing the national anthem and salute the Cuban flag.

Even though a 1991 reform allowed Christians to join the CCP and prohibited religious discrimination, systematic discrimination persists. Many Christians remain reluctant to join the CCP, viewing it as promoting an anti-religious ideology. Christians often experience limited opportunities, including being overlooked for promotions, excluded from important meetings, demoted, or transferred to undesirable locations because of their faith and non-CCP membership.

Members of the Cuban security agencies, including the military and the police, who choose to convert to Christianity face specific discrimination. After leaving the CCP, these individuals report being visited and threatened by party officials with potential repercussions for them or their family members.

Despite some easing of restrictions on participation in religious activities by members of Cuban security agencies, reports of discrimination continue. Young Christians fulfilling their compulsory military service are singled out for intense harassment or subject to particularly rigorous exercises.

Furthermore, the Cuban government through the ORA and the Ministry of Housing, severely restricts the construction of new church buildings. Only a limited number of new churches have been approved since 1959. With the rapid increase in practicing Christians in Cuba, this severely violates their religious liberty as many are prohibited from freely congregating for worship.

The government did make an announcement after the Pope's 2012 visit that the Catholic Church would be allowed to construct a few new buildings. However, this right has not been extended to other religious groups, thereby creating a situation of religious inequality rather than freedom. Non-Catholic religious groups in Cuba have expressed deep concern about this development and continue to demand that the government establish legal mechanisms to streamline and regularize the application process for building or renovation permits for all religious groups.

Church Property Destruction

Faith organizations in Cuba are continually under threat, with multiple reports of church property being targeted for demolition. This has been an ongoing issue across the island, particularly in rural locations. Churches connected to the Apostolic Movement seem to be particularly frequent targets of theseincidents. One such case from December 29, 2021, involves Dámaris Marín, wife of Pastor Bernardo de Quesada. She was informed by Leonel Risco de Franco, the director of the Housing

Authority, that an outdoor terrace used for religious activities on their property must be demolished, contradicting previous assurances from the city authorities. When Marín went to retrieve the legal documents, she had received earlier, she discovered that the records of her submission were missing.

A significant incident involved the Baptist Church in Yaguajay, housed in a historical pre-1959 building that was once the Baptist High School. The church was notified in April 2012 that the property was supposedly nationalized in October 1980. The leadership believes the church was targeted due to their refusal to comply with government demands. Local authorities claimed the Ministry of Education had given the property to two government businesses, ESPROT and GEOCUBA. The land was repurposed shortly after the church was informed.

Restrictions on Public and Social Ministry

The right to public manifestation of faith is crucial to most church groups, yet it is severely regulated by the government. This permission is not universally granted but is only extended to certain groups for specific events. Religious processions and evangelistic work are rarely permitted. There have been some recent exceptions, like public Masses held during Pope Benedict XVI's visit and a Methodist Church revival in the town of Santa Lucía.

Despite these exceptions, many religious groups claim that the government's control over granting authorization for public events remains stringent. Even Freemasons, who are also under the Office of Religious Affairs' jurisdiction, have reported that they are routinely denied permission to hold public parades. Also, most of the formal requests to hold public events frequently go unanswered.

Those who conduct public activities without permission face severe consequences. A group of pastors and church leaders in Bayamo, eastern Cuba, were subjected to fines, physical abuse, and arrests while distributing gospel tracts at a bus station and conducting public evangelism. In February 2021, Pastor Juan Moreno was beaten severely, resulting in his hospitalization. Several other pastors who protested these actions were also detained and coerced into signing 'pre-arrest' documents.

Government's Limitations on Social Ministry

Numerous religious groups in Cuba participate in social ministries, such as the distribution of food, medicine, clothing, and services for the elderly. However, these endeavors often face government restrictions. The government views these activities as a threat, particularly when local agencies are unable to provide these services.

However, the impact of Hurricane Sandy in late 2012 resulted in a slight relaxation of these restrictions. Some denominations reported being allowed to receive and distribute donations under strict government supervision.

Scarcity of Religious Materials

Christian leaders have persistently voiced their concerns over the severe shortage of Bibles and other religious literature, an issue particularly prevalent in rural areas and significant in cities as well. This problem, based on reports from faith organizations working in Cuba, affects all denominations, including Protestants and Catholics both within and outside the CCC. The shortage is largely attributed to rigid government constraints on the import of religious materials and limited access to printing infrastructure. For example, in Protestant denominations, all religious literature including Bibles must be imported under the CCC's authority, which only represents a minority of Protestant Christians. Catholics also face difficulties in importing Bibles and sometimes have to work with the CCC to bring Bibles into the country.

Limited Access to Media

Unless they are specifically authorized, Cuban and joint ventures cannot sell computers, fax machines, photocopiers, or other equipment to any church except at official, inflated retail prices. Furthermore, many religious organizations are denied Internet access, creating a virtual state monopoly on printed media. Any church organizations or independent organizations with access to a printing press are heavily scrutinized.

The closure of the Center for Religious and Civic Formation in Pinar del Rio and the termination of publications Vitral and Bifronte are speculated to have been due to intense governmental pressure on church hierarchy. The government continues to exert control over the editing of Catholic publications. Nevertheless, some publications, like Palabra Nueva in Havana, have managed to publish articles and commentary critical of government policy and have become an important part of the independent press.

Religious leaders across all the denominations express dissatisfaction with the continued lack of media access. This issue is aggravated by the perception that state media gives easier access to Afro-Cuban religions under the guise of their activities being cultural rather than religious. Some exceptions have been noted, such as televised events linked to Pope Benedict XVI's visit and occasional broadcasts granted to the CCC and some of their member denominations. However, faith organizations working in Cuba regard this selective granting of media rights as promoting religious inequality, not religious freedom.

Religious Rights of Political Prisoners

In September 2009, the government announced that it would allow Protestant and Catholic religious services in Cuban prisons. However, no provision was made for non-Christian faiths. The initial responsibility for Protestant services was assigned to a CCC pastor, which was met with criticism since the CCC represents only a small fraction of Protestant Christians in Cuba. Nonetheless, Reverend Francisco Rodés made an effort to include all denominations in the training required for government approval to carry out prison ministry.

Despite positive developments, many concerns raised by church leaders regarding the reform's implementation appear to have been justified. The government retains the power to arbitrarily bar specific pastors from involvement in prison ministry. The execution of this right to hold religious services varies across prisons, with some outright denying services, while others interrupt or cancel them even midcourse.

Most political prisoners continue to be barred from participating in these services. Authorities often claim that only 'well-behaved' prisoners can attend, arbitrarily excluding political prisoners. In other cases, participation in religious services is contingent upon wearing the prison uniform, which most political prisoners refuse to wear on grounds of conscience.

In 2021, Protestant Christians Ulises Lacaba and Jeikel Peña Díaz, held in the 'El Pre' Prison for Youth in Santa Clara, were arbitrarily denied the right to participate in official religious services. Following an attempted complaint by Lacaba, he was beaten, sent to a punishment cell, and held in isolation for an extended period. Disturbingly, other prisoners report that he was treated so badly that he attempted suicide.

Inmates continue to report being arbitrarily denied the right to pastoral visits, worship, prayer, and study meetings with other prisoners. They also report frequent confiscation of Bibles and other religious literature, sometimes as punishment or for no apparent reason, an issue particularly problematic for political prisoners.

Security Climate

Cuba's restrictive environment primarily stems from the government's strong enforcement of communist principles. Through the use of Decree Law 370 (implemented on July 4, 2019), which curtails freedom of speech (Freedom House, May 6, 2020), and Decree Law 35, government officials persistently threaten and levy fines on dissidents and activists. This includes Christians, who regularly confront surveillance, interrogations, and arrests by various state and non-state actors committed to the Communist Party's ideology.

One example of these non-state actors are the Committees for the Defense of the Revolution (CDRs), community-level groups that effectively function as domestic surveillance networks. They watch and report on the activities, relationships, and histories of their neighbors, providing crucial information to the police and other state agencies.

Multiple internal and external intelligence agencies, including the Department of State Security (DSE), the General Directorate of Intelligence (DGI), the Directorate of Military Intelligence (DIM), the Directorate of Military Counterintelligence (DGCIM), and the National Revolutionary Police (PNR), work in concert to maintain the ruling party's grip on power. Both psychological pressure and physical violence are used without consequence against those who oppose the Communist Party's rules.

An additional form of abuse includes anonymous complaints lodged by the "State Security Organs" (OSE) to intimidate critics of the regime

(Cuba Trendings, May 6, 2021). This includes confining potential regime opponents for prolonged periods in sealed vehicles exposed to the sun, a tactic referred to as "patrulla-horno" (Connectas, June 2021).

Following the July 11, 2021 protests, the International NGO Observatory for Human Rights (Observatorio) recorded 1745 oppressive actions in Cuba, with 1103 being detentions and 642 comprising other abuses (OCDH, August 3, 2021). Observatorio reported that there were 414 acts of repression in September 2021 alone, with 79 incidents of arbitrary detainment. Other offenses against human rights activists, journalists, or independent artists involved house raids, harassment, police summonses, threats, fines, and attacks by the police.

Institutions like the Inter-American Commission on Human Rights (IACHR), including its Special Rapporteurs for Economic, Social and Cultural Rights (REDESCA) and Freedom of Expression (RELE) have condemned the Cuban government for its repression and use of force during the July 11 protests (OAS, July 15, 2021).

Furthermore, Cuba is both a source and transit country for human trafficking, primarily affecting women and adolescents. The US State Department's 2021 Trafficking in Persons report found that the Cuban government failed to investigate, prosecute, or convict trafficking crimes and didn't report identifying victims.

Christians are among those most affected by the governmental repression. During July 2021, multiple priests and pastors were subjected to arbitrary detention and injury (Cope, July 14, 2021). The police confiscated the crosses of some detained Christians (Vida Cristiana, July 14, 2021), and a protester holding a poster with the words "Long live Christ the King" was held in custody.

Trends in Cuba's Repression of Freedom of Religion and Belief (FoRB)

The marked deterioration in respect for religious freedom in Cuba is alarming. The government appears to be cracking down on any groups potentially advocating for social and political reforms. While the Pope's visit in March 2012 and subsequent promises by the government to grant privileges to the Catholic Church were seen as signs of a renewed commitment to religious freedom, the reality proved different. Both

Catholic and Protestant churches across all denominations reported serious violations of religious freedom weekly.

At this time of exceptional hardship for the Cuban people, the government has clamped down on civil liberties. Monitors continue to document and report on religious freedom violations with familiar patterns of regime abuse, including detentions, arrests, destruction of church buildings, confiscation of faith community property, travel restrictions, and deprivation of rights to social services, employment and education.

The UK-based religious freedom advocacy organization CSW documented 272 cases of FoRB violations in 2021. In response to the July 11 protests and the increasing use of online platforms to criticize the regimes policies, on August 17 the regime issued Legal Decree 35, masked as a "cybersecurity" law, that criminalizes any online criticism of the government and incitement to public disturbances. These decrees are inspired by recent laws in Russia that have been used to control the Internet, identify sources of anti-government content, and wield political control. The authoritarian playbook has also been used in Nicaragua where the Sandinista-controlled National Assembly passed two similar laws used by the Ortega-Murillo regime in May and June 2021 to imprison all seven of the leading opposition candidates before the November presidential elections which the international community has branded as fraudulent.

The Castro regime has consistently misled the international community regarding its commitment to human rights improvements. It's crucial that the international community, including the European Union and the United States, not be deceived by the Cuban government's gestures of granting limited privileges to specific religious groups. Any improvement in religious freedom should be universal and grounded in legal systems and protections without discrimination or favoritism.

Emerging Multi-Faith Unity

In recent years, the faith community has presented a more unified front. Churches of different faiths, historically and intentionally divided under the Cuban government's religious "caste system" and repression by the government's watchdog, ORA, are increasingly working together to defend religious freedom and basic human rights, and openly advocating for the common good. By the very nature of these roles, the faith community has become the single most effective voice of the independent civil society that the Cuban government works so hard to exclude. Although not sanctioned by the government, new faith alliances involving Catholics, evangelicals and some unregistered churches are providing an alternative platform to the government's tightly controlled interfaith platform, the CCC.

In the last three years, a number of faith alliances have emerged, though their growth has been limited by regime repression and the COVID-19 lockdown. They share a commitment to constructive and peaceful dialogue and long-term reforms:

- Alliance of unregistered inter-denominational religious groups/churches. This group represents the most victimized faith group due to its having no legal recognition. The post-July 11 crackdown has increased pressure against its members, and many received citations or threats during the period.

- Catholic Alliance (Aerópago Cubano). This alliance has various community levels of engagement. Through social media and messaging apps its visibility has grown among Cubans. Drawing on Catholic Social Doctrine, its members publish regular thoughtful political and socioeconomic critiques. As a result, several of its members, including priests, have become targets of defamation and harassment campaigns.

- Another example of interfaith cooperation, in the aftermath of July 11, is a dynamic association of Catholic and Protestant church leaders called Cristianos Cubanos en Comunión (C3). In 2021 the members of C3 coalesced around a shared common vision, including Christian evangelization and a collective "search for liberty, truth and goodness." The group held a large National Day of Prayer for Cuba on October 10, 2021, and continues to hold virtual prayer events that draw participants from the island as well as other countries in the region.

Current Situation

Cuba faces numerous crises including social, economic, and

political challenges, leading to shortages of food, medicine, and fuel, exacerbated by the ongoing COVID-19 pandemic. Additionally, frequent power outages, inadequate healthcare, education, and have aggravated the hardships faced by Cubans.

In 2022, religious freedom conditions in Cuba deteriorated. The Cuban government tightly controlled religious activity through surveillance, harassment of religious leaders and laity, forced exile, fines, and ill-treatment of religious prisoners of conscience. Religious leaders and groups not abiding by the strict regulations set out by the Office of Religious Affairs (ORA) were relentlessly oppressed. This oppression escalated to the point of many religious leaders leaving Cuba in 2022 to seek asylum.

A direct consequence of these crises has been the rise in criminal activities driven by desperation. With limited opportunities for self-employment, instances of drug trafficking and robberies have increased, creating heightened insecurity among the population.

Enhanced State Oppression Amidst Social Unrest

The intensification of social critique, driven by the regime's failures and the deteriorating living conditions, has bred greater rebellion within the Cuban populace. Regardless of the government's intimidating tactics, the Cuban people's call for basic liberties and drastic reform to the existing governing model has become resoundingly louder. When the citizens diverge from the government's agenda, they face escalated repression from the authorities and their allies.

Rising Hostility Towards the Church

In response to Cuba's escalating crisis, church leaders have been more vocal in criticizing the government, turning the church into a regular target of government animosity. On one hand, defending the most vulnerable and engaging in communal activities among various church denominations has bolstered unity and respect within communities. However, on the flip side, it has also drawn the ire of the government and triggered increased scrutiny and attempts to control.

As the challenges mount, religious leaders and communities both within and outside Cuba are stepping up to mitigate the harsh conditions confronting the country.

They're developing strategies to deliver humanitarian aid, resilience programs, and spiritual guidance to those affected. Still, these efforts often encounter roadblocks and repression from the Cuban government.

The government has shown a growing intolerance towards dissent and religious groups outside the officially recognized Council of Churches in Cuba. These groups frequently face obstacles in performing pastoral or aid-related activities, often aimed at supporting vulnerable populations. Furthermore, the recent reform of the Penal Code poses a new threat by allowing the authorities to punish individuals or organizations receiving foreign funding for perceived anti-government activities. This development puts faith-based organizations at risk of being labeled as dissidents, even when their work solely focuses on humanitarian aid.

Increasingly, religious institutions have also become targets for robbery and vandalism. The frequency of church break-ins mirrors the overall surge in violence across the country. In some instances, these attacks seemingly target religious leaders who openly criticize the government's policies. This creates a particularly hostile environment for religious communities.

This precarious situation highlights the mounting failures of the current regime and illustrates the perils religious entities face when they divert from the government's ideology. The persecution of the church not only affects religious communities but also undermines the support they offer to the broader population, which heavily depend on their aid.

Despite these hurdles, religious organizations remain unwavering in their commitment to addressing the needs of the Cuban people. They persist in advocating for human rights and condemning government malpractices, even amidst adversity. Their work offers a crucial lifeline for those impacted by the ongoing crisis, providing a beacon of hope in these trying times.

Section III
Nicaragua: One of the Worst Violators of Religious Freedoms

"The international community must know and realize that this government belongs to a transnational criminal organization… which, by remaining in power under the facade that everything is normal, has sentenced Nicaraguans to the silencing of their voice through death, exile or banishment, and prison. Currently, it has eliminated more than3,126 social organizations, has taken over all the movable and immovable property of these organizations, applies laws at its convenience and eliminates those who interfere with maintaining its totalitarian power. Today the population lives under a state of siege, fearful, as all the rights inherent to the human being are violated. Nicaragua has become a prison state … for its people. The government achieves subjugation through the use of armed force. Faced with this, the people issue an SOS to anyone who can help Nicaragua."
--David, religious freedomdefender in exile

Introduction

In recent years, Nicaragua, once a country revered for its respect for religious freedom, has witnessed a significant decline due to the stringent authoritarian regime of President Daniel Ortega and his FSLN party. With a wave of citizen protests that began in April 2018, the state's recognition and protection of religious liberties have been significantly diminished. Escalating government and paramilitary assaults targeted primarily the Catholic Church, especially during the contentious 2021 general election campaign. Ortega, aided by his wife and Vice President, Rosario Murillo, manipulated the electoral process and seized a new five-year term through a sham vote count in November. This move provoked widespread international condemnation.

Despite the government's successful attempts to suppress independent NGOs, media outlets, and dissident voices, Nicaragua's churches and other faith organizations persist, bravely opposing political repression and human rights violations.

Religious Repression Under the Ortega Regime

Inaugurated again on January 2022, President Daniel Ortega and Vice President Rosario Murillo, representing the Sandinista National Liberation Front (FSLN), now firmly control Nicaragua's National Assembly. Under their governance, especially from November 2021 to November 2022, both human rights abuses and FoRB violations have intensified.

Religious leaders advocating for human rights or expressing dissent face increasing threats, ranging from verbal harassment to potential violence and unwarranted detention. These intimidating tactics lead many religious leaders to practice self-censorship. As reported by CSW, a seemingly innocent sermon on topics like unity or justice might be misconstrued as a direct critique of the government, warranting punitive measures. Many religious leaders and followers, including foreign citizens and native Nicaraguans, have been forcibly exiled, barred from re-entry, or arbitrarily detained. Notably, the imprisonment of Roman Catholic priests surged in the latter half of 2022.

Additionally, Nicaraguans have been forbidden from publicly displaying religious symbols like crucifixes, the Star of David, or banners symbolizing peace, justice, and democracy. The state further restricts political prisoners' access to religious literature, including Bibles.

2022 saw an alarming increase in attacks against civil society organizations (CSOs), including those of religious affiliations, being stripped of their legal statuses by the National Assembly. This has resulted in numerous shutdowns, government property confiscations, and forced exiles of faith community members. The government also escalated its efforts to prohibit public religious gatherings, such as outdoor worship services and processions. Pro-democracy activists, human rights advocates, and political opposition members were continuously harassed by state security forces, often being warned against affiliating with faith communities or participating in religious ceremonies.

The Ortega regime perceives churches and their followers as threats to its stability. This viewpoint has spurred the government's relentless intimidation, surveillance, and attacks against them. Regardless, the faithful remain unyielding, publicly condemning the government's rampant human rights abuses. In particular, during electoral periods, Christian leaders continue to advocate for the rule of law and provide aid to those marginalized, including those opposing the dominant Sandinista Party.

In this section of the book, we delve deeper into the deterioration of religious freedom from 2018 to 2022 and propose actionable recommendations for the U.S. Government and the global community. The objective is to bolster Nicaragua's faith community in its vital role in the nation's prospective reform process.

Historical Background

Nicaragua, a country with a turbulent history, oscillated between dictatorship and democratic phases over the past century. Its modern political saga began in 1936 under the iron-fisted rule of the Somoza family which lasted until 1979 when the Sandinista National Liberation Front (FSLN) toppled their reign. Daniel Ortega emerged as a prominent figure in this era, taking up the presidential mantle first from 1984 to 1990, and then again in 2006, holding the reins of power until the present.

The country's constitution, particularly in Article 69, robustly underscores the right to religious freedom. It guarantees the right of all individuals to express their religious beliefs, be it privately or publicly. This right is safeguarded unless it infringes upon the law or obstructs others from exercising their rights or duties.

The promise of democracy, however, was slowly eroded as Ortega and Murillo strengthened their hold on power since 2007. With the backing of their political party, the FSLN, they stifled opposition, manipulated legislative norms, and entrenched themselves at the pinnacle of Nicaraguan politics. In a move that further consolidated their grip, the National Assembly, under the FSLN's dominion, abolished presidential term limits in 2014. Consequently, Ortega's prolonged rule was received strong international criticism, notably when the Organization of American States (OAS) condemned the 2021 presidential elections as lacking 'democratic legitimacy.'

Unyielding, the Ortega-led government distanced itself further by withdrawing from the OAS later that year.

Years in power revealed a transformation in Ortega. Once a revolutionary, he increasingly mirrored the dictatorial tendencies of the leaders he had once opposed. Despite an exterior of stability, underneath lay a bubbling cauldron of weak rule of law, rampant corruption, and repression. This simmering discontent boiled over in 2018 when the populace protested changes to the pension system. The Roman Catholic Church, in its role as a mediator, found itself in the crosshairs as it extended help to protesters. The government's retaliation was swift and fierce: media campaigns against the Church, assaults on places of worship, and a blatant disregard for religious rights.

The government's apathy was also evident in its handling of the COVID-19 pandemic, as it neglected to implement preventive measures, thereby risking public health. In this backdrop, some Protestant leaders who expressed solidarity with the protests faced the government's wrath. Pastor Wilber Alberto Pérez's arrest in December 2020 exemplifies this.

A brutal crackdown ensued in response to the 2018 protests. The Inter-American Commission on Human Rights (IAHCR) documented a harrowing tale of violence, torture, and abuse, concluding that the Nicaraguan state's actions amounted to crimes against humanity. This brutal suppression of civil liberties continued with the introduction of the Special Cybercrime Law in 2020, a stark reflection of the government's escalating control over freedom of expression.

As the 2021 elections approached, the political climate turned even more volatile. Not surprisingly, Ortega clinched another term, but not without international rebuke. Amidst the tumult, the exodus of Nicaraguans seeking safer shores surged dramatically. Between 2021 and 2022, the U.S. reported detaining a significant number of Nicaraguans, and the UN Refugee Agency (UNHCR) noted a spike in asylum seekers in neighboring Costa Rica.

This historical overview paints a picture of a nation grappling with its ideals, its leadership, and the aspirations of its people. Through it all, the struggle for religious freedom stands as a testament to Nicaraguans' enduring spirit.

Nicaragua's Faithful Majority: Religion and Politics in a Changing Landscape

Nicaragua, steeped in a rich history of religious fervor and faith, has constitutionally enshrined the principle of freedom of religion. Up until 2010, concluding the second term of President Daniel Ortega, the government was generally perceived to respect religious freedom. In 2005, the U.S. Department of State's International Religious Freedom report lauded the Nicaraguan government for promoting the free practice of religion and fostering an atmosphere of interfaith harmony.

However, as the years rolled on, the religious demographics of Nicaragua witnessed a considerable shift. An M&R Consultants survey in 2017 reported that Catholicism, once the predominant faith, now accounted for 46 percent of the believers, while Evangelical membership surged to 33 percent Notably, 14 percent identified as faithful though non-affiliated. By 2019, a study by Borge and Associates documented a further growth of Evangelical Protestants to 41 percent with a dip in Catholics to 43 percent. The remaining smaller religious communities, including Jews, Muslims, and others, made up less than two percent of the population. Interestingly, the Pew Research Center estimated the Muslim community to be around 1,000 in 2010, while the Israelite Congregation of Nicaragua suggested a Jewish population between 70-100.

Despite repeated assertions by the U.S. State Department regarding a clear demarcation between church and state in Nicaragua, historical ties suggest otherwise. The Somoza dynasty, which ruled prior to the Sandinista era, cultivated a relationship with the Catholic Church. The church's leadership was expected to abstain from politics in exchange for freedom to expand their religious missions and educational institutions. The Vatican, in line with its approach towards ensuring stability in Latin America, overlooked the autocratic tendencies of leaders like the Somozas. Yet, this did not deter a faction of Nicaraguan priests, troubled by the mounting inequalities and human rights transgressions, from supporting the Sandinista revolution in 1979. Post-revolution, the bond with the church became even more evident when a few priests took up governmental roles, clashing with the Vatican's insistence on political neutrality.

Ortega's Oscillating Affiliation with Catholicism

Ortega, during his initial years, identified as a Leninist and was often in the company of Sandinista atheists. But, given the significant Christian presence within the revolutionary movement and the intrinsic religiosity of Nicaraguans, outright atheism was never a widespread Sandinista policy. The 1969 party policy even went on to guarantee religious freedom.

2006 marked a turning point for Ortega, as he publicly reaffirmed his commitment to Catholicism, notably under the guidance of Bishop (later Cardinal) Obando y Bravo. This religious pivot was further underscored when Ortega rallied support in the National Assembly for a stringent anti-abortion law, a gesture that cemented his bond with the Catholic clergy. The Ortega family's regular appearances at mass services were a testament to their newfound religious allegiance.

However, this association was transient. Ortega eventually distanced himself from Catholicism, labeling the church as adversarial. Instead, the family gravitated towards the rapidly expanding Evangelical church. This shift was palpably evident when Ortega's son, Laureano Ortega Murillo, along with his spouse, attended an evangelical service in 2019, an event widely covered by state-controlled media. Observers and former allies have critiqued Ortega's religious switch as purely tactical. Henry Ruiz, an ex-Sandinista guerilla, remarked that Ortega employed "religion as a tool of ideological domination." Echoing similar sentiments, former deputy Eliseo Nunez sarcastically commented that for Ortega and his wife, Rosario Murillo, consolidating power could mean converting "even to Scientology."

The April 2018 Revolt and the Onslaught on Religious Institutions

Before the widespread protests of April 2018, there were already signs of the Nicaraguan government's interference in religious practices and its mounting aggression towards independent churches that stood up for the human rights of the Nicaraguan people. During the 2011 presidential campaign, the FSLN intertwined religious faith with its revolutionary platform, coining the slogan "Christianity, Socialism, Solidarity." This deliberate melding of religious imagery and political intent intensified over the years. By 2013, mandatory Christian values education had been introduced into the school system. A year later, a family law was enacted, putting community Family Committees, which were under the control of the FSLN, in charge of promoting Christian values and, more controversially, exerting control over Catholic religious festivities.

But the government's overreach didn't stop there. Increasing reports from various religious communities highlighted governmental harassment against them, especially if they voiced opposition to official policies. Numerous administrative challenges were created, ranging from withholding essential benefits for religious activities to the delayed customs clearance of imported church supplies. This suppression, in the guise of bureaucratic hurdles, escalated to new regulations on religious travelers, often missionaries, in 2016. The government cited concerns about illicit activities, such as drug trafficking, as a reason. But in reality, it was another veiled attempt to curb religious freedom and control external influences. Over time, the government escalated its retaliation against religious groups and civil society organizations it viewed as antagonistic, even going so far as to block the registration of faith-based organizations and churches.

Though the U.S. State Department had been monitoring the decline of religious freedom in Nicaragua, it often noted the absence of "societal actions" hampering religious freedom. However, everything changed in April 2018. A proposal for austerity measures targeting social security triggered large-scale public protests. The government's brutal response to these peaceful protests was swift and severe. In the following weeks, hundreds of Nicaraguans, a significant portion being students, faced incarceration, death, or simply vanished. This violent repression, coupled with the stifling of any form of dissent, threw the nation into chaos. Nicaragua's economy nosedived as investors grew wary, and a significant portion of its citizenry sought refuge in neighboring countries.

August 2021 brought a grim report from the Nicaraguan Center for Human Rights (CENIDH), which documented escalating hostility from the government towards the Catholic Church. Instances of vandalism, such as the arson attack on Managua's Immaculate Conception Cathedral, which destroyed a centuries-old image of

Jesus, became alarmingly frequent. Clergy spoke of regular harassment from both the police and pro-government groups, especially after services that prayed for political prisoners.

Faith leaders who had offered sanctuary and medical aid to protesters in 2018 continued to face consequences, ranging from slander to unwarranted investigations and fabricated charges. Measures such as cutting utilities to churches of dissenting priests and revoking the permits of educational and medical institutions run by anti-government clerics showed the lengths the government would go to suppress the religious community. Even funerals weren't spared, with government supporters disrupting these solemn events and vandalizing the final resting places of pro-democracy protesters.

In mid-2022, a report by Nicaraguan attorney Martha Patricia Molina for the Observatorio Pro Transparencia y Anticorrupción detailed a staggering 190 attacks on the faith community since 2018. This encompassed various forms of aggression, from graffiti on church walls and threats against Catholic clergy to bureaucratic barriers against Catholic NGOs and explicit hostility towards priests by Daniel Ortega and Rosario Murillo.

A telling incident occurred in December 2021, when Nicaragua severed ties with Taiwan and recognized the People's Republic of China. Taiwan's attempt to gift its former embassy building to the Managua Catholic Archdiocese was thwarted by the Ortega government, further emphasizing its tightening grip on both political and religious fronts.

Ortega's Assault on Civil Society and Freedom

In the wake of the citizen-led protests of April 2018, Ortega escalated his repression against civil society. Before this, Ortega had employed more subtle tactics to keep the populace under control, but the post-protest period saw him resorting to more overt, and oftentimes brutal, forms of repression.

Numerous CSOs, some of which had been beneficiaries of grants from the U.S. Agency for International Development (USAID) and other international donors, found their registrations revoked. Their leaders were detained, and their assets seized. Ortega's strategy to dominate public discourse was evident in his acquisition of media outlets. Over the past two decades, Ortega and Sandinista allies have consolidated control over the majority of radio, television, and print outlets. This near monopoly allowed the government to control the narrative. Following the 2018 protests, Ortega intensified his crackdown on the few independent media outlets that remained. Numerous outlets were forcibly shut down, journalists were persecuted, and some even lost their lives in the process. For instance, in the first four months of 2022 alone, the Association of Independent Journalists and Communicators in Nicaragua recorded a staggering 175 government violations of freedom of expression.

Ortega's onslaught wasn't limited to the press. International NGOs, which collaborate closely with local entities, also faced obstacles. They encountered problems like the obstruction of imported relief goods, new mandates to register as foreign agents, and a widespread deregistration campaign that impacted 163 NGOs. After the controversial 2021 elections, Ortega's regime further tightened its grip. Since the 2018 protests and up to June 2022, over 400 local NGOs had been shuttered. The National Assembly implemented reforms to increase control over universities, given that students from these institutions had been active protestors in 2018.

Many of the targeted NGOs were actively involved in human rights, social welfare, cultural, and developmental endeavors. The legislative branch supplemented Ortega's tactics by passing additional restrictive laws, such as cybercrime and sovereignty laws, and modifying existing legislation to further restrict NGO activities.

Given the global emphasis on the role of civil society in the democratic process, one wonders about Ortega's endgame. Cuba offers an example where the government has set up proxy organizations to give the illusion of a thriving civil society. It's not entirely clear whether Ortega intends to replicate this model, but certain indications suggest he might. The Inter-American Commission on Human Rights has noted the use of community-based Citizenship Power Councils (CPCs) and Sandinista Leadership Committees (SLCs) by Ortega's regime. These entities, which operate at the grassroots level, have morphed into tools of surveillance and control.

Post-2018, CPCs have been instrumental in identifying and monitoring those deemed as "enemies of the state." The SLCs, on the other hand, have ensured that government employees participate in state-sanctioned activities and have kept an eye on those who might not align with the government's ideology. This level of surveillance undeniably links the actions of CPCs and SLCs with the violent repression executed by paramilitary groups against civil society and religious organizations.

Political and Legal Landscape

Nicaragua's ruling Socialist party, the FSLN, has centralized power to a degree that has raised significant concerns among international human rights and democratic institutions. The party's dominance has expanded to control not just the executive branch but also the electoral, judicial, legislative powers, and extends to police, the military, and even municipal leadership.

Despite the presence of opposition, particularly the National Coalition formed in 2018 comprising seven political and civil organizations, their lack of unity has hindered their ability to challenge the Ortega regime effectively. This was evident during the presidential election on November 7, 2021.

Embedded corruption and the establishment of a legal framework that seemingly legitimizes human rights restrictions and abuse of power have further solidified the regime's control. Such legislative measures have eroded the right to peaceful assembly, association, and have reduced electoral credibility. Notably, the legislative assembly, dominated by the Ortega faction, introduced laws that:

1. Block financing to civil society organizations perceived as "disruptive."
2. Impose life imprisonment for ambiguously defined "hate crimes."
3. Penalize spreading of "false news" on social media.
4. Prevent anyone labeled as a "traitor to the homeland" from running for public office.

These laws were further bolstered by electoral reforms that curbed the participation of the opposition, threatening the transparency and credibility of the electoral process. This paved the way for various repressive actions like the arrest of eight presidential candidates and the intimidation and harassment of perceived opponents.

The international community has expressed serious concerns about Ortega's policies. These concerns, however, have been dismissed by Ortega, who has rejected international condemnation as interference. Despite these dismissals, the Inter-American Commission of Human Rights (IACHR) and the UN High Commissioner for Human Rights (OHCHR) for Central America and the Dominican Republic have been proactive in voicing their concerns about the deteriorating state of human rights in the country.

International Response

In response to the Ortega administration's actions, multiple nations have imposed sanctions aimed at promoting human rights and facilitating a democratic transition. The U.S., Canada, the European Union, and other Latin American countries have targeted individuals and entities associated with the Nicaraguan government.

Civil society organizations, including Human Rights Watch, International Crisis Group, Freedom House, and Amnesty International, have also been active in highlighting the government's human rights violations.

The Role of the Church

Amidst the political turmoil, the church, especially the Roman Catholic Church, has emerged as a beacon of hope and resistance. It has played an active role since the social unrest began in April 2018. Initially participating in dialogue between the government and opposition groups, the Catholic Church withdrew in 2019 due to the regime's continuous human rights violations.

While the Church has been vocal in its support for the vulnerable, this has led to its portrayal as a 'public enemy' by the government.

Consequently, church leaders, buildings, and faith-based organizations have faced retaliatory actions, ranging from disinformation campaigns to physical threats and attacks.

Despite facing considerable adversity, the Church has continued to advocate for a transparent electoral process, democratic values, and respect for human rights. Their efforts during the November 2021 elections included raising awareness, promoting transparency, and condemning political persecution.

Threats and Harassment

The year 2022 saw an unsettling rise in religious freedom violations. Dominantly orchestrated by government officials, these violations were also perpetuated by pro-government activists and paramilitary groups. In many instances, both forces worked in tandem to suppress religious freedom.

Take, for instance, the case of the San Juan Bautista Roman Catholic Church in Masaya. On May 14, church authorities were alerted about a civilian probing into the whereabouts and schedule of their parish priest, Harvin Padilla. Within a day, the church premises were virtually under siege, with heavy police surveillance and the presence of officers in riot gear. This tension reached its zenith on May 16, when a paramilitary group was stationed nearby, along with an overwhelming police presence in and around the church vicinity. Concerned for his safety, church leaders decided to relocate Father Padilla to a safer location in Managua. However, their fears were justified when, on September 5, unidentified men sought information about the relocated priest.

This is far from an isolated incident. Religious communities often faced ongoing harassment and threats, with some intensifying even after their leaders stepped down. One church in the South Caribbean Coast Autonomous Region (SCCAR) provides a poignant testament to this. The church's pastor experienced persistent surveillance by hooded men, instilling such fear in him that he refrained from visiting the church for months.

A Strategic Shift to Evangelicalism

The rift between President Ortega and the Catholic Church deepened after the events of April 2018. As Catholic clergy provided refuge to citizens opposing the government, Ortega retaliated by targeting Catholic leaders and their establishments. In a bid to counterbalance this deteriorating relationship, the Ortega-Murillo administration fostered closer ties with Evangelical leaders. Despite protests from some Protestant and Evangelical figures against state repression, the administration deemed them as potential allies. Notably, the rapid growth of Evangelical churches in Nicaragua influenced the government's pivot towards Evangelicalism.

The state, under Ortega's leadership, displayed a unique method of favoring religious institutions. Between 2007 and 2018, churches, religious foundations, and the Catholic university, UNICA, received nearly $20 million in aid. The majority of these funds were aimed at aiding the Catholic church in preserving historical religious sites, like the Cathedral of Leon, which was granted over $1 million. The association between Ortega and figures like Cardinal Obando y Bravo and the ex-President of the Supreme Electoral Commission (SEC), Roberto Rivas, further explains this allocation. Significantly, 43 percent of this budget, roughly $600,000 annually, was allocated to UNICA.

However, according to the NGO Nicaragua Investigates, by 2018 there was a noticeable increase in grants directed at numerous evangelical Protestant groups, which comprised 12.5 percent of the total multi-year budget. A vast majority of the religious entities that received funding between 2007-18 were identified as Evangelical. The transparency regarding the usage of these funds remains questionable.

In October 2019, 67 pro-government Evangelical pastors were awarded property titles. This initiative was a continuation of the government's efforts to legalize properties for Evangelical churches, with 853 properties having been legalized from a pending 2,000 requests. Furthermore, Evangelical churches received funding designated for National Assembly members. The Ortega-Murillo government funded various biblical projects across cities. Commenting on this trend, sociologist Maria Teresa Blandon observed, "numerous government efforts to legalize properties for Evangelical churches, with 853 properties having been legalized from a pending 2,000 requests. Furthermore, Evangelical churches received funding designated for National Assembly members. The Ortega-Murillo government funded various biblical projects across cities. Commenting on this trend, sociologist Maria Teresa Blandon observed, "numerous government officials behave as though they were Evangelical pastors."

This section of the book underscores the pressing need for international oversight and intervention to safeguard the rights and freedom of the Nicaraguan populace.

The Socialist Authoritarian Paradigm

The tactics adopted by the Ortega-Murillo regime in Nicaragua follow a distinct playbook, echoed by nations like Russia, Cuba, Venezuela, and occasionally other members of the Bolivarian Alliance. The core objective of these nations is to exert dominant Socialist state control over their citizenry. Such governments frequently masquerade their authoritarian actions under the guise of international security initiatives.

The global fight against terrorism, especially as outlined in the UN Global Counter-Terrorism Strategy, is a frequent justification. This strategy emphasizes the enhancement of national, regional, and international counter-terrorism measures. It ranges from fortifying state defenses against terrorist threats to better coordinating UN System counter-terrorism activities. Key proponents of such measures have traditionally been the U.S. and European nations.

However, nations like Russia and its Socialist allies in Latin America have contorted the term "terrorism" to encompass political opposition and independent civil society organizations. They've implemented severe measures under the pretext of "protecting" state interests. Russia's branding of opposition figure Aleksei Navalny as a "terrorist and extremist" is a case in point. Similarly, before its military incursion into Ukraine, Russia criminalized the spread of "fake news" concerning its military operations, effectively muzzling opposition. Such laws and strategies, touted as anti-terrorism measures, are in fact designed to suppress civil society and opposition, curbing democratic practices.

In 2020, Nicaragua introduced a "foreign agents' law," wielded against political opponents and civil society groups. Pitched as an anti-terrorism tool, this law prevents those labeled as "foreign agents" from financially supporting or participating in Nicaraguan politics, and from seeking public office. Subsequent legislation, like the Special Cyber Crimes Law and Act 977, curtailed freedom of information and enforced financial transparency for NGOs. Though these are touted as means to curb terrorism, their actual purpose is to restrain civil society operations and activities.

The Climate of Repression

In 2021, global human rights watchdogs, including the UN High Commissioner for Human Rights, raised alarm over deteriorating human rights conditions in Nicaragua. The escalating repression included arbitrary arrests, assaults, and surveillance, curbing the rights to freedom of peaceful assembly, association, and expression.

Reports from organizations such as Human Rights Watch and the U.S. State Department painted a bleak picture of Nicaragua's rights scenario. These reports detailed the extensive overreach of the police and other national security forces, including arbitrary detentions and politically motivated persecutions.

The Ortega government, in its bid for absolute power, has often enlisted police, parapolice groups, and vigilantes (dubbed "Ortega squads") to clamp down on perceived opposition. Despite international censure, the government remains unyielding in its stance and denial of human rights abuses.

Church leaders and religious groups, primarily Catholics, became significant targets for the regime, especially when they voiced opposition to the government's actions or narratives. This severe crackdown further intensified as the 2021 elections loomed.

Global Response to Nicaragua's Repression

Following the contentious elections in November, the international community increased scrutiny and sanctions on the Ortega-Murillo regime.

As Daniel Ortega began this latest term in January, several global powers including the U.S. and the European Union imposed sanctions on key Nicaraguan officials and entities.

The incarceration and mistreatment of political opponents, especially leading presidential candidates, drew sharp criticism. By March 2022, the number of political prisoners in Nicaragua stood at 181. The grave conditions they faced, including reports of torture, inadequate medical care, and isolation, drew international ire.

Nicaragua's alignment with Russia, particularly during the Ukraine crisis of 2022, further complicated the nation's global standing. With Russia as a significant donor, the impacts of global sanctions on Russia also reverberated in Nicaragua. As a result, essential aid and funding programs faced uncertainty, underscoring the intricate geopolitics at play.

Religious Intolerance and International Scrutiny in Nicaragua

Nicaragua's violation of religious freedom has been a significant concern on the global stage. The U.S. Department of State's International Religious Freedom reports have frequently criticized the nation's handling of religious matters. In 2019, at the recommendation of the U.S. Commission on International Religious Freedom (USCIRF), Nicaragua was added to the Special Watch List of severe religious freedom violators, joining Cuba as the only countries from the Western Hemisphere.

The UN Human Rights Council (UNHRC) voiced its concerns in June 2021 with a resolution titled "Promotion and Protection of Human Rights in Nicaragua." The resolution highlighted governmental restrictions on public spaces, repression against civil society, human rights defenders, and religious leaders.

The Observatory for Religious Freedom in Latin America (OLIRE) recorded numerous instances where religious freedoms were infringed. These include assaults on the Catholic Masaya mission, the defacement of a Catholic shrine in Estelí, and denial of entry to Nicaragua to two clergy members.

Shockingly, violent actions against religious institutions, especially Catholic ones, jumped from nine in 2019 to 26 in 2020 and slightly decreased to 21 in 2021. Such actions include verbal and physical violence, smear campaigns, death threats, arbitrary arrests, and unending surveillance. Places of worship frequently face vandalism, forcing the religious community to establish protective measures against desecration.

In its 2023 annual report, Freedom House noted that Nicaragua experienced the second largest decline in freedom over the past 10 years, with only Libya seeing a larger decline. Notably, since 2018, the government has not allowed any international rights monitoring bodies into the country. The government's restrictive stance extends beyond human rights to sectors like poverty, food security, and health.

Catholic Leaders as Beacons of Hope

Post the 2018 uprising, Catholic leaders and clergy have showcased immense bravery. They not only provided refuge to the persecuted but also stood as vocal critics of governmental human rights abuses. Catholic churches, such as the Blood of Christ Chapel of the Managua Cathedral, faced direct attacks. Still, leaders like Cardinal Leopoldo Brenes, Managua's Auxiliary Bishop Silvio Baez, and Monsignor Carlos Avilés continued their advocacy.

Several bishops, such as Monsignor Rolando José Alvarez, Monsignor Jaime Ramos, and Monsignor Miguel Mantica, have been broadcasting messages on respect for human rights, non-violence, and the essence of a free society through Catholic-run media outlets. They do so in a climate where independent media is being silenced or forced into exile.

However, their advocacy hasn't gone unnoticed. The government, led by Ortega and the FSLN, has often branded these religious leaders as "terrorists and traitors to the nation." Still, any drastic measures against the Catholic Church are checked given the influential stance of the Vatican in international politics.

Challenges Faced by the Evangelical Community

The Evangelical community, unlike the Catholic Church, is diverse and decentralized. After the 2018 crackdown, some criticized

Evangelical churches for not providing refuge like their Catholic counterparts. However, many Evangelical leaders argue that their silence should not be misinterpreted as alignment with the government's views.

These independent Evangelical leaders lack the protection of a central authority, making them more vulnerable to direct governmental actions. Their grievances include long-pending land title requests and revocation of licenses of Christian media outlets critical of the government.

The Divide in Interfaith Unity

Daniel Ortega and Rosario Murillo have masterfully maneuvered the religious landscape, shifting alliances from Catholicism to Evangelical Christianity for their benefit. True religious freedom benefits from the unity of all religious voices, especially in places where some faiths face restrictions. In Nicaragua, the chasm between Catholics and Evangelical Protestants has been widened due to Ortega's repressive tactics. Until this divide is bridged, achieving true religious freedom in the nation remains a distant dream.

Current Situation Throughout the recent years, the Nicaraguan government has adopted tactics to instill fear within the Catholic community. Several priests have been expelled, prevented from returning to the country after international trips, with no formal explanation provided. A notable case was in March 2022 when the government unexpectedly revoked the credentials of Monsignor Waldemar Sommertag, the papal nuncio in Managua since 2018, forcing him to depart. Similarly, Father Juan de Dios García received an email notification from the Directorate General of Immigration and Nationality, stating he was prohibited from re-entering Nicaragua after a family visit to the U.S. The regime further denied Father Guillermo Blandón re-entry after his travel to Israel.

This tension escalated when Ortega, in a televised speech, criticized the Church, calling it a "perfect dictatorship," and rehashed accusations against the clergy as "killers" and "coup plotters." In December, he further charged them with inciting violence during the 2018 protests.

The abuse perpetrated against Bishop Rolando Álvarez epitomizes the government's crackdown on the clergy. Known for mediating in the 2018 national dialogue and critiquing the government's human rights offenses, Álvarez found himself under police surveillance by May. In response, he sought sanctuary in a Managua church and initiated a hunger strike. Although police later permitted his return to his Matagalpa diocese, his vehicle was escorted throughout the two-hour drive. By August 5, the national police declared an investigation against the bishop, subsequently raiding his church, detaining him, and charging him with conspiracy, spreading misinformation, and maligning the government. Vice President Murillo rationalized these actions as necessary for preserving Nicaraguan family peace and security. By February 2023, a court had sentenced Bishop Álvarez to 26 years imprisonment, alongside stripping him of his citizenship.

Simultaneously, seven men were arrested, including three priests, one deacon, two seminarians, and a layperson. They were sentenced to a decade in prison for charges including conspiracy and disinformation but were later exiled to the U.S. along with other political detainees.

Analyzing the State of Affairs

1. International Denunciation of the Ortega Regime: As democracy eroded and the rule of law disintegrated leading up to the November 2021 elections, the international community, alongside human rights bodies, expressed their disapproval of the Ortega regime. The Vatican has consistently voiced its support for Nicaraguan Christians.

2. Escalating Repression of Dissent: With potential extension of Ortega's presidency in the horizon during the November 2021 elections, the regime amplified its crackdown on critics, with the Church bearing the brunt of this hostility.

3. Rampant Corruption: Ortega's tenure has seen increasing corruption. From misusing public funds for party propaganda to collaborating with unlawful factions, the government has intensified Nicaragua's existing crises and inequalities. Consequently, those considered regime adversaries, such as the Church, are left vulnerable.

Conclusion

The human rights landscape in Nicaragua between November 2021 and 2022 is deeply alarming. The government's intrusive surveillance and intimidation, particularly of religious groups, suggest an intention to wipe out independent civil society, mirroring Cuba's strategy. As such, Nicaragua is witnessing a historically unparalleled migration wave, reminiscent of Cuba in the 1990s.

Despite international criticism, the Nicaraguan government remains unyielding. Strengthened ties with other countries with questionable human rights records might reduce its receptivity to global pressures. This stubbornness reveals the government's perception that its most significant threat is internal.

To restore democracy and human rights in Nicaragua, the international community must devise ingenious strategies to fortify independent civil societies, both domestically and in exile. Simultaneously, safeguarding the intertwined rights of freedom of religion, expression, assembly, association, privacy, non-discrimination, and others, is crucial.

Increasingly, bodies like the UN Special Rapporteur on Freedom of Religion or Belief, the OAS, the IACHR, and numerous global human rights watchdogs are intensifying their focus on Nicaragua. Their involvement is paramount to shield smaller human rights defenders and activists.

The importance of religious unity in times of religious freedom assaults is evident from Cuba's experience, where governmental divide-and-rule strategies have fragmented the faith community. Yet, the rising cooperation among churches, even across denominations, offers a ray of hope.

Lastly, Nicaragua has evolved into a precarious territory for human rights advocates and development partners. Any externally backed initiatives need to prioritize the safety of both implementers and local collaborators. The government's continued and aggressive attempts to quell opposition, independent societies, and external supporters underlines the urgency of this need.

I conclude this section of the book by quoting Felix Maradiaga, a Nicaraguan human rights defender and political leader:

"Ortega is imprisoning all religious leaders and any church that raises its voice in favor of the people and against the dictatorship. He wants to give countries abroad the impression that everything is in order and that there is no problem in Nicaragua. Internally, he oppresses the vast majority of the people who live without information due to poverty. Very few have access to social networks because they cannot cover the costs since the little that is earned daily is [dedicated] to the survival of their family. The dictatorship dominates the radio and television media, the private cable networks. It has eliminated religious channels and radio stations little by little. It has done the same thing with private radio stations in order that what is really happening in the country goes uncovered. All of this, the socio-political and economic situation, has led to extreme poverty and the great departure of thousands of Nicaraguans into exile."

Section IV
Venezuela: A Breach of Freedoms

Introduction

Venezuela, once Latin America's crowning jewel of democracy and prosperity, now stands as a harrowing testament to how rapid decline in governance can lead to a surge in poverty, food scarcity, economic downturns, and human rights violations. The very fabric of the nation has unraveled, with millions fleeing in search of better prospects, leaving behind a beleaguered populace grappling with dwindling resources, compromised healthcare, rampant violence, and an ever-looming threat of crime.

While the international community, encompassing donor organizations, Non-Governmental Organizations (NGOs), and faith-based entities, strives to alleviate the mounting pressures within Venezuela, their efforts are often hampered by the prevalent violence, political instability, and a government that views external intervention with suspicion and hostility. However, the beacon of hope remains in the form of Local Faith Organizations (LFOs), notably the Catholic Church and the burgeoning Evangelical Protestant denominations. These entities, despite government barriers, are tirelessly addressing the humanitarian crisis at the grassroots level. Yet, with over 24 million people trapped in dire poverty within Venezuela's borders, the pressing need is for the government to collaborate with these local faith organizations, facilitating enhanced assistance and recognizing them as pivotal in the nation's reformative journey.

Legal Framework

The Venezuelan constitution, while protecting religious freedom, sets forth that religious practices should not undermine public morality, decency, or order. A 1964 concordat, a bridge between the government and the Holy See, earmarks funds for Catholic educational institutions. Yet, in 2017, the contentious National Constituent Assembly (ANC), which many view as illegitimate, instituted an anti-hate law. This law, comprising 25 articles, criminalizes any incitement to hatred or violence, leading to prison sentences ranging from 10 to 20 years. It encompasses an extensive range of prohibitions, from political activities to individual acts and media transmissions that propagate hatred or violence. Notably, this law makes no concessions for religious discourse.

The Directorate of Justice and Religion (DJR), an arm of the Maduro-led Ministry of Interior, Justice, and Peace, undertakes the responsibility of religious group registrations, liaison functions, and disbursement of funds to religious entities. For a religious group to gain legal recognition, it must register with the DJR. This process mandates disclosures relating to property ownership, clergy identification, and the group's foundational principles. Moreover, to gain registration approval, these groups must illustrate their commitment to social services within their communities and secure acceptance letters from the regime-approved community councils. However, approval from the ministry remains arbitrary, with potential indefinite delays.

While the law remains neutral on the inclusion of religious education in public schools, an existing agreement between the Episcopal Conference of Venezuela (ECV) and the state permits Catholic teachings in public institutions. This is primarily geared towards imparting sacramental values and preparing students for First Communion. Nevertheless, adherence to this agreement remains inconsistent.

Furthermore, provisions exist to cater to the spiritual requirements of Catholic military personnel through appointed chaplains. Similar provisions for other religious denominations remain absent. Venezuela, in its commitment to upholding civil and political rights, is a signatory to the International Covenant on Civil and Political Rights.

Regime Practices and Interventions in Religious Activities

In various instances, the regime leveraged the anti-hate law, designed ostensibly to curtail "fascism, intolerance, or hatred," against religious figures. The most striking case occurred when Father Alfredo Infante, a prominent Jesuit leader in Venezuela, faced legal repercussions from

Carabobo State's United Socialist Party of Venezuela (PSUV)-affiliated governor, Rafael Lacava. This was a direct result of Centro Gumilla's contribution to PROVEA's annual human rights report that highlighted a troublingly high number of extrajudicial killings in Carabobo.

The Catholic Church consistently expressed concerns about the political and humanitarian crises unraveling within Venezuela. Archbishop Jesus Gonzalez de Zarate and Cardinal Baltazar Porras were vocal advocates for societal healing and open communication between the political leaders and citizens.

Despite the Church's peaceful endeavors, representatives noted a halt or reduction in funds to Catholic schools, predominantly serving impoverished regions. This financial cutback seemed to be the regime's attempt to curb the church's influence and activities. In addition to the funding issues, the church faced bureaucratic challenges, such as difficulties in procuring religious visas for their clergy.

Furthermore, a disturbing revelation emerged in June 2022, as reported by the Washington Post. Numerous priests who were convicted of child or adolescent sexual abuse either did not serve their sentences or served abbreviated ones. Some even resumed their clerical duties post-conviction. This raised concerns about systemic impunity within the nation.

Regrettably, the Jewish community also found itself in the regime's crosshairs. Notably, PSUV vice president Diosdado Cabello utilized derogatory rhetoric, substituting the term "Jewish" with "Zionist", in a veiled attempt to stoke antisemitism.

Regime's Dubious Political History

Under Nicolás Maduro's leadership since 2018, the country has experienced controversial and disputed electoral processes. Despite international and national outcry over the legitimacy of his leadership and the National Assembly elections, Maduro and his allies continue to solidify their grasp over the nation. Juan Guaidó's stint as the self proclaimed interim president, though supported by many countries, unfortunately did not yield a democratic transition.

The various dialogues between the government and opposition

delegates have been unstable, and the opposition is now strategizing for the 2024 general elections. However, Chavismo's iron grip over the nation's institutions persists, leading to the continued erosion of the rule of law, hostility towards the opposition, and systemic human rights violations. Highlighting the depth of these violations, the International Criminal Court began investigations into the egregious human rights abuses stemming from the 2017 opposition protests.

The deterioration of the Venezuelan political landscape has severely impacted basic human rights, economic stability, and the overall social fabric. A study by the Andrés Bello Catholic University of Caracas showed a spike in poverty rates and a reduction in educational coverage. The media, an essential pillar of democracy, also suffered under the regime's repression, with biased election coverage and targeted actions against independent outlets.

This oppressive climate contributed to a mass exodus from Venezuela, with UNHCR reporting around 7.13 million Venezuelan refugees and migrants globally.

Religious Communities as Beacons of Hope

In these trying times, the religious community in Venezuela emerged as a ray of hope, transcending their primary spiritual roles. They not only criticized the regime's transgressions and advocated for transparent electoral processes but also launched initiatives to improve living conditions for Venezuelans. From sanitation drives to food security campaigns, these faith-based interventions aimed to offer a semblance of dignity and hope to the beleaguered populace.

An Unprecedented Economic Collapse

The U.S. Congressional Research Service (CRS) paints a bleak picture of Venezuela's multiyear economic crisis, noting it as "one of the worst in the world." Since 2014, the economy has shrunk by over 75 percent, a collapse that stands unparalleled in 45 years, dwarfing even the severity of the U.S. Great Depression. By 2019, hyperinflation skyrocketed to an astounding 10 million percent, effectively reducing the currency to a mere token.

Venezuela's dependence on imports for consumer goods is glaring, with a nearly 95 percent drop since 2013. This decrease has led to drastic shortages of vital food and medicine. Unfortunately, the country has continued to favor irrational economic strategies despite repeated warnings from the International Monetary Fund and the wider global community. A litany of desperate measures—from developing an oil-based cryptocurrency to seeking credit from traditional allies like Russia and China—have come up short.

Historically, Venezuela's wealth has been closely tied to its vast oil reserves, mirroring the global shifts in petroleum prices. Under the leadership of President Hugo Chávez in the early 2000s, a significant portion of this oil revenue was funneled into social welfare programs. However, the nationalization of private businesses led to disruptions in the economy and dwindling private investments. Despite Chávez's passing in 2013, his successor, Nicolás Maduro, clung to a similar economic approach, plunging Venezuelans into deep economic strife, rampant corruption, and oppressive politics.

By January 2019, questions of Maduro's legitimacy came to a head, with nations like the U.S. no longer recognizing him as the rightful leader of Venezuela. Yet, broad sanctions and military interventions were met with skepticism and concerns for the already suffering Venezuelan populace.

Abysmal Living Conditions

The domestic conditions in Venezuela are dire. Recent surveys highlight that 96 percent of the population lives under the poverty line, a sharp increase from the 2014 figures. Nutrition is a significant concern, with one in three Venezuelans facing food insecurity and increasing rates of child malnourishment. Basic amenities, such as potable water and electricity, have become luxuries. Diseases, once eradicated, are resurfacing, and the health infrastructure is on the verge of total collapse. The already burdened health system now grapples with the COVID-19 pandemic, with limited access to vaccines. In many regions, the government has seemingly abdicated its responsibilities, allowing criminal organizations to fill the void.

The need for humanitarian assistance is palpable. USAID estimates that seven million Venezuelans, including vulnerable groups such as pregnant women, children, and the elderly, urgently need aid.

Challenges for Displaced Venezuelans

The challenges of the pandemic extend beyond domestic borders, complicating the plight of Venezuelans seeking refuge abroad. Gasoline shortages mean many have to undertake grueling journeys by foot, seeking assistance from NGOs and church groups. Closed borders due to the pandemic have driven people to use illegal crossings, often controlled by criminal outfits demanding exorbitant bribes.

Migratory Exodus and International Assistance

The ripple effect of Venezuela's crisis is felt throughout the region, with neighboring countries grappling with a significant influx of Venezuelan migrants. The U.S., too, has seen a surge in refugees, with many traversing through Central America and Mexico. Despite the magnitude of the crisis, many migrants find themselves in limbo, lacking official status and vulnerable to exploitation and abuse.

A Government Against Its People

In 2020, UN High Commissioner for Human Rights Michelle Bachelet indicted the Maduro government for a slew of human rights violations, from extrajudicial killings and torture to widespread political repression. The government's hold on power is bolstered by foreign support, with Cuban military and intelligence agencies playing a key role in training and supporting Venezuelan forces. The International Criminal Court, recognizing the gravity of these violations, is considering launching a comprehensive investigation.

In this grim landscape, the fight for freedom and human rights is of paramount importance. The resilience and courage of those standing against these oppressive forces offer a glimmer of hope for a brighter future for Venezuela.

Religious Freedom in Venezuela: An Overview

Venezuela, a primarily Christian nation, boasts a significant Catholic population, making the Catholic Church one of its oldest and most entrenched institutions. It remains the only religious institution with full legal status. Other prevalent Christian groups include the Evangelical Council of Venezuela, the Venezuelan Evangelical Pentecostal Union, the Network of Christian Churches of Venezuela, the Church of Jesus Christ of Latter-Day Saints, and Jehovah's Witnesses. Additionally, minority religious communities like Jews, Baha'is, Muslims, Buddhists, and indigenous religious groups contribute to the country's diverse faith landscape.

However, the journey for religious freedom in Venezuela has been a rocky one. Evangelical churches have long sought the same recognition that the Catholic Church enjoys. Yet, the Directorate of Justice and Religion (DJR) has burdened them with capricious registration prerequisites. This discrimination leads to prolonged registration delays for these churches, restricting their operational abilities.

Constitutional Protections and Limitations

The Constitution of the Bolivarian Republic affirms religious freedom and worship, with certain constraints related to morality, public order, and ethics. It pledges church independence and endorses parents' rights to select religious education aligning with their beliefs.

But there's a contradiction. The Venezuelan Penal Code penalizes religious ministers who publicly scorn national institutions or laws. Further, the ambiguously worded "Law against Hate for Peaceful Coexistence and Tolerance" can, and has, been wielded to quash dissent, stifling freedom of expression.

Governmental Interference and Bias

Recent policies showcase the government's attempt to tighten its grip over religious entities. One prominent move was establishing the Vice Presidency of Religious Affairs of the United Socialist Party of Venezuela (PSUV). Headed by the president's son, Nicolás Maduro Guerra, this body aims to assimilate Christian groups within regional and local governance. Their strategy involves forming Government Pastoral Councils countrywide, further integrating these Christian factions into the government's machinery. Though pitched as support for religious entities, these measures seem more like strategies for control.

The government's alliance with certain evangelical factions has led to preferential treatment, including facilitations like faster registration and enhanced access to public services. This bias has sparked concern among other religious communities, wary of the government's intentions and the potential erosion of religious freedom.

Religious Leaders: Advocates and Adversaries

Religious entities in Venezuela aren't just about faith; they play an essential role in social activism. Leaders, particularly from the Catholic Church, have been vocal critics of the government, championing transparent elections and human rights, and providing humanitarian aid amidst the ongoing crisis. This activism hasn't been without consequences. Religious leaders have been detained, threatened, and even attacked for their stance.

Political Ideology and Religion: The Intersection

Venezuela's ruling party pushes for communist ideology, where state and society adhere to its guidelines. This approach has permeated educational institutions, restricted academic autonomy and imposing a specific worldview on students. This ideology also perceives certain religious teachings, particularly from the Catholic Church, as subversive, leading to tensions and reprisals against religious entities.

The Menace of Organized Crime

Organized criminal entities, including local and international gangs, pseudo-unions, and drug traffickers, are alarmingly influential in Venezuela. Their operations intersect with state agencies, casting a shadow over the country's governance. These groups present significant challenges to religious freedom, as they exert control over territories, indoctrinate youth, and pose threats to religious leaders advocating for peace and human rights.

Venezuela's Religious Demography

Estimates suggest that as of midyear 2022, Venezuela had a population of around 30 million. However, the Inter-Agency Coordination Platform for Refugees and Migrants posits that the figure may be considerably less, considering the migration of over seven million citizens since 2015.

According to the most recent statistics, 96 percent of Venezuelans are Catholic, although this number is believed to be decreasing due to the rise of evangelical Protestant communities and the nonreligious. Non-Catholic demographics include evangelical Protestants, members of the Church of Jesus Christ of Latter-day Saints, Jehovah's Witnesses, Muslims, and Jews.

It's worth noting that many individuals practice Afro-descendant religions, like Santeria and Spiritism, in conjunction with Christianity. The Muslim community, primarily of Lebanese, Syrian, and Libyan descent, estimates its followers to be between 100,000 and 150,000, with the majority being Sunni. The Jewish community has witnessed a decline from 30,000 members in 1999 to an approximate 10,000, most of whom reside in Caracas.

Venezuela's Evolving Religious Landscape

Venezuela, historically a Catholic stronghold, has witnessed shifts in its religious landscape. Recent estimates from the Episcopal Conference of Venezuela (ECV) suggest that Catholics make up about 67 percent of the populace, evangelical Protestants 18 percent, non-affiliated religious believers 10 percent, with the remaining 4 percent comprising various other religious groups.

The Catholic Church's dominance is waning, giving way to an increasing number of evangelical Protestant churches. The broader trend across Latin America indicates a decline in Catholic affiliations. According to Pew Research, only 59 percent identified as Catholic in 2017, down from 92 percent in 1970. This change is attributed to a significant portion of former Catholics joining Protestant churches.

The Catholic Church's Diminished Leadership Role

Churches have historically played pivotal roles in addressing humanitarian crises across Latin America. In Venezuela, the Catholic Church, given its vast institutional presence, has actively addressed the nation's challenges. Despite its respected standing, the Church's capacity to initiate political change remains symbolic. The Church's influence is limited, especially in enforcing political resolutions.

Rise of Evangelical Protestants in Venezuela

Parallel to a decline in Catholicism, there's been a surge in the number of evangelical Protestants. The past few decades have seen the Evangelical community grow from a meager 3 percent to an estimated 20 percent of the religious population in Latin America. The success of evangelical churches is often attributed to their emphasis on values-based discourses and family support.

Local evangelical organizations within Venezuela have been addressing various aspects of the crisis. Organizations like Corazones de Esperanza (CDE) have been particularly active, operating community kitchens, managing storage facilities, and distributing humanitarian goods to vulnerable populations. With aspirations to expand its outreach, CDE serves as a beacon of hope in tumultuous times.

Venezuela's Assault on Religious Freedom and the Political Use of Religion

The Political Manipulation of Religion

Maduro regime has strategically intertwined religion and politics. In 2020, it introduced the National Religious Council (NRC), a move that many saw as an attempt to control religious narratives. The regime consistently sought the support of the Evangelical Christian Movement for Venezuela (MOCEV), a pro-Maduro entity. The fact that President Maduro celebrated the "National Pastor Day" with MOCEV is telling of the relationship.

In 2022, a controversial "Good Pastor" Plan was announced, urging the registration of evangelical Protestant churches via the Government Pastoral Councils, a system expanded by the regime in 2019 in alliance with MOCEV. Joining this system came with financial incentives, further deepening the intertwining of church and state. The Evangelical Council of Venezuela (ECV) expressed its reservations about this system, emphasizing that it diverged from the principles held by many evangelical Christians in the nation.

In the same vein, an attempt was made in 2021 to push a law requiring NGOs, including religious organizations, to be part of a regime-controlled registry for foreign donations. This move was seen by many as an attempt to control and limit foreign influence. Although this proposal didn't become law, it showed the lengths the regime was willing to go to control the narrative.

The Assault on Religious Freedom

Religious freedom, essential for a democratic society and a robust civil society, is under threat in Venezuela. Although the U.S. Commission on International Religious Freedom (USCIRF) has not placed Venezuela on any of its lists of concern since 2009, developments in the country in recent tell a different story.

The Jewish community in Venezuela, although small, has faced indirect threats, with the government historically using anti-Semitic rhetoric. The U.S. Department of State highlighted significant concerns regarding religious freedom in 2021. Despite a constitutional promise of freedom of religion, leaders from the Catholic Church and the Evangelical Council reported harassment and intimidation by the regime for their outspokenness on the country's crises.

The government's actions have not been limited to verbal intimidation. Physical threats and attacks on churches, congregants, and religious leaders have been documented. Disturbingly, pro-Maduro media have employed anti-Semitic tropes, trivializing tragedies like the Holocaust, even linking the Jewish community to the COVID-19 pandemic.

These orchestrated attacks have led to tangible fear within religious communities. Churches were burglarized, precious religious artifacts stolen, and religious leaders faced physical threats for their work. Incidents such as the Nazi-themed birthday party in Caracas in 2022 highlight the growing boldness of anti-Semitic sentiment.

Despite these challenges, the independent Venezuelan Interreligious Forum continues to operate, seeking dialogue on human rights, democratic values, and rule of law. Faith-based organizations have played a pivotal role, not only addressing the humanitarian crisis but also standing as one of the remaining beacons of an independent civil society in the country.

Venezuela: Struggling for Religious Freedom and Human Rights

Regulation of Churches

In 2021, the Venezuelan government introduced the Administrative Ruling N ONCDOFT-001-2021, forming the foundation for the Regulations for the Unified Registry of Obliged Subjects before the National Office Against Organized Crime and Terrorism Financing (RUSO-ONCDOFT). These ruling mandates both national and international non-profit civil entities based in Venezuela to enlist with the ONCDOFT. The implications are significant: not only must these organizations disclose their donors, but also the recipients of their charitable endeavors. Additionally, member details are required, with an underlying presumption of involvement in illicit activities such as terrorism.

Various civil society organizations and the Inter-American Commission on Human Rights (IACHR) have vehemently opposed this regulation. They argue it jeopardizes the safety of individuals protected by these organizations, infringes on the right to freedom of association, and violates the principles of innocence until proven guilty.

Of particular concern are organizations dedicated to human rights and church-affiliated social action groups. These bodies fear serious repercussions. Activities or members even slightly associated with activities the government deems threatening or terrorist-like could be sanctioned, stigmatized, or face other oppressive actions.

Violence Against Christian Leaders

Venezuela has witnessed an alarming rise in targeted attacks on Christian leaders and sacred places. Between 2020 and 2022, numerous religious leaders have been assassinated and many places of worship vandalized.

A tragic example is Brother Luigi Manganiello, the principal of the La Salle religious institute. After attempting to thwart a robbery at his school in January 2021, he succumbed to resulting injuries. Similarly, in January 2022, the remains of Angel Isaac Ortega Romero, a 19-year-old catechist, were discovered a year after his disappearance.

His murder, it seems, was retaliation for him reporting thefts at his workplace. Furthermore, in October 2020, Father José Manuel De Jesús Ferreira was fatally shot resisting a robbery attempt outside his home.

These incidents underscore not just the general violence plaguing Venezuela, fueled by local criminal groups and external entities like Colombian guerrillas, but also the nexus some of these groups share with the Venezuelan government. The rampant lawlessness places religious leaders in a perilous position.

State Interference: The Pastoral Government Council

The concept of a secular state is fundamental to guaranteeing equal treatment for all religious beliefs and practices. It ensures the autonomy of religious entities and safeguards them against state intervention.

However, since 2019, the Maduro regime has blurred these boundaries by expanding the reach of the "Pastoral Government Council." Composed of evangelical pastors handpicked by local officials, the council aims to bridge the efforts of the state and evangelical churches.

Its responsibilities are manifold, including policy formulation on 'permissible' religious practices, church and pastor registration, and even theological training for Christians. However, these measures have raised concerns among various Christian communities. The Evangelical Council of Venezuela, representing a significant Christian demographic, expressed its unease regarding the potential ramifications of such state-initiated census and registrations, especially the "Good Shepherd Bonus," which grants financial aid exclusively to registered pastors.

The council stresses the significance of the separation of Church and State, contending that state efforts to amalgamate the myriad voices within the Venezuelan evangelical community runs counter to its core values.

Religious Entities as Peacemakers

On September 14, 2022, OLIRE and the University of Costa Rica's Chair of Education for Peace held a webinar titled "The Role of

Religious Communities in Promoting Conflict Resolution," in which experts from Colombia, Mexico, and Venezuela discussed the historical and present roles of religious communities in their respective nations.

Dr. Andrés Felipe Arbeláez, Deputy Director of Religious Freedom and Conscience Affairs at the District Secretariat of Government of the Mayor's Office of Bogotá, stressed the multi-faceted roles religious bodies play, from child welfare to environmental conservation. Dr. Diana Katherinne Cardona Garzón, Coordinator of the Observatorio Socioeclesial Actualizando Shalom (OSEAS) of Justapaz Colombia, emphasized the Mennonite Church's contributions to peace talks and conflict resolution in Colombia.

Dr. Victor Manuel Brenes from Mexico showcased the "National Strategy for the Promotion of Respect and Tolerance for Religious Diversity," a peace-building initiative. Lastly, Dr. Juan Salvador Perez of Venezuela elaborated on the evolving relationship between the Catholic Church and the government, emphasizing its pivotal role in diplomacy and peace-building efforts.

The takeaway is clear: While religious freedom faces challenges in Venezuela, religious communities are striving to be a beacon of hope, peace, and resilience in challenging times.

Interfaith Cooperation Inside Venezuela

In light of Venezuela's ongoing government repression, the country's faith community has unified to emphasize its essential role in humanitarian aid. Established in April 2020, the Foro Interreligioso Social (Interfaith Social Forum) was born with the mission of addressing the pressing societal challenges eroding family values, community ties, living conditions, and democracy itself. Notably, they've petitioned the government to allow the World Food Program to begin operations, particularly given the surge in food insecurity due to the pandemic.

Leadership of the Forum includes a representative from the Episcopal Conference of Venezuela (ECV), the Conference of Catholic Bishops, and a representative from the Protestant churches. Furthermore, it has a triad of spokespersons representing the Catholic Church, Protestant churches, and evangelical churches. Last year, the Forum took proactive steps to augment its humanitarian reach by sending three members for training at the University of Barcelona. Regrettably, financial constraints have hindered the full deployment of their new skills upon return.

This Forum stands in contrast to the government-aligned Consejo Interreligioso Compuesto (Consejo), which, similar to Cuba's Cuban Council of Churches, created by the Cuban government to control a select group of approved religious institutions, the Consejo consists only of government-registered non-profit churches. Other churches are systematically sidelined, depriving them of the legal standing necessary to function, and leaving them more vulnerable to repression.

In Venezuela, the typically splintered evangelical community is also witnessing unprecedented unification. Alliances such as the Venezuela Evangelical Council, Union of Venezuelan Christian Churches, and the Pentecostal Confederacy of Venezuela exemplify the budding spirit of interfaith collaboration to champion religious freedom and progressive reform.

Intimidation and Harassment of the Humanitarian Community

The Maduro regime consistently undermines the international humanitarian community. Their tactics range from raiding NGO offices and arresting staff to imposing challenging bureaucratic obstacles. This has made delivering aid within Venezuela incredibly challenging. Recently, the Maduro government introduced an added layer of bureaucracy, mandating NGOs to register with its Office Against Organized Crime and Terrorism Financing. Such restrictions have dire consequences, worsening the ground reality, heightening risky migrations, and forcing the international community to redirect their resources mainly to assist refugees.

In the wake of such impediments, the UN Office for the Coordination of Humanitarian Affairs (OCHA) remains committed to negotiating with the Maduro regime, striving for renewed cooperation to alleviate the severe crisis that plagues Venezuela.

Restrictions on NGOs and Civil Society

Human Rights Watch interprets the NGO suppression as the government's sustained assault on Venezuela's already fragile independent civil society. Recent regulatory changes are concerning, requiring NGOs to provide sensitive information that amounts to direct governmental oversight. Furthermore, the recent actions of the National Assembly to curtail civil society organizations signal an increasingly hostile environment.

Current Events

In 2022 and 2023, the Venezuela Affairs Unit, which is housed in the U.S. embassy in Bogotá, persisted in its commitment to engaging with the interim government and independent civil society. They maintained robust communication with diverse religious groups, emphasizing the repression of religious communities and antisemitic content in various media.

Conclusion

Venezuela's alarming descent into a humanitarian crisis and political corruption and authoritarianism over the last several years presents an alarming study in the erosion of basic freedoms and rights. The stranglehold of an authoritarian regime coupled with mounting economic and social pressures paints a grim picture. Yet, in these trying times, the resilience of local faith organizations and the continued efforts of the international community offer a glimmer of hope. It underscores the importance of continued international vigilance, collaborative efforts, and the relentless pursuit of re-establishing Venezuela's democratic foundations.

Religious freedom, a cornerstone of liberal democracy, has been severely compromised in Venezuela, despite constitutional assurances. Faith leaders face intimidation for highlighting the country's humanitarian turmoil, and religious institutions have been targeted. The Maduro regime's actions, both towards the international humanitarian community and local NGOs, especially faith-based ones, limit their capability to assist the Venezuelan populace, compounding the national crisis.

While the religious landscape of Venezuela continues to evolve, the role of religious institutions remains crucial. They not only provide spiritual guidance but also play a significant role in humanitarian efforts, addressing the multifaceted challenges the nation faces.

Furthermore, the regime's consistent use of antisemitic propaganda and its broader targeting of various religious communities' paints a concerning picture for religious freedom in Venezuela.

Venezuela's journey towards true religious freedom is fraught with challenges. While the constitution promises liberty, on-the-ground realities tell a different tale. The intertwining of religion, politics, and crime makes for a complex landscape where the fight for freedom becomes multifaceted. Religious leaders and institutions remain at the forefront, battling for their rights amidst this turmoil.

Section V

Faith versus Greater Social Impact

On August 3, 2023, Pastor David Lorenzo Rosales Fajardo, sentenced to a seven-year term in a Cuban prison on charges including assault and battery, incitement to commit a crime, public disorder, and unlawful disobedience," successfully passed on an urgent message from his confinement. His crime? Daring to condemn the unjust

---

Theme: The Christian and Politics
Can a Christian go into politics?

"The only thing necessary for the triumph of evil is that good men do nothing."
(Edmund Burke)

Speak up for those who cannot speak for themselves, for the rights of all who are destitute.
Proverbs 31:8 - New International Version

Based on the Text from Daniel 6: 1-4
1It pleased Darius to appoint 120 satraps to rule throughout the kingdom, 2with three administrators over them, one of whom was Daniel. ...
\----------------------------
Are Christian ideals and practices compatible with the activities of political government? It is true that the subject is very complex, since it has many edges, and we will try to reflect on it.

Let's look at the inspiring example of the prophet Daniel. How interesting! How wonderful!

A man of God, who is at the peak of power, an environment in which men generally lose their minds, and allow themselves to be seduced by luxuries, vices, and pressures of all kinds, as well as selfish ambitions; at the same time, he is so blameless in his conduct that not even his own enemies can find any fault or vice with which to accuse him.

We could also speak of Joseph in Egypt, of Moses as governor of the people of Israel, also of King David, of his son Solomon; today we have many modern believers, that is, of our time, who hold government positions.

In the New Testament, we find John the Baptist. What did John the Baptist preach? Luke 3:10-20

10"What should we do then?" the crowd asked.........

JESUS CHRIST: (Jesus accuses the scribes and the Pharisees)
Matthew 23:13-29
Seven Woes on the Teachers of the Law and the Pharisees
13"Woe to you, teachers of the law and Pharisees, you hypocrites! You shut the door of the kingdom of heaven in people's faces. You yourselves do not enter, nor will you let those enter who are trying to........

---

arrest of his 11-year-old son. Now he hoped to rouse the collective consciousness of the global Christian community.

Summary

For many Christians today, the world we live in seems utopian, since there are so many petty economic and political interests that give us the feeling that no one can access or remain in power without being corrupted, or without being "removed" from power because it bothers them.

But what I want to highlight here is the principle of what is legitimate, of political activity for the Son of God. From there to whether it is feasible is another matter.

But in case you feel called to a political vocation, or you are exercising it, remember that the key to continue being a Christian in any position, is that like Daniel, be faithful to the last, blameless, and that far from strengthening with your life the idea that "every man has his price", you can show that by the Grace of God, you are incomparable, and that you are there only to contribute to the welfare of society, and not to satisfy selfish personal interests, and show a JUST AND GOOD GOD, TO THE KING OF KINGS AND LORD OF LORDS.

Pastor David Lorenzo Rosales

In this message, he emphasizes the divine mandate that requires Christians to step forward for the oppressed and the voiceless. This obligation to show compassion and love towards their fellow human beings is bestowed upon Christians by God Himself. Unfortunately, this profound duty is not comprehensively grasped by the Christian faithful or by the churches they belong to. It is a matter of urgent necessity that Christians understand this call to service, enabling them to make significant strides in the realm of human rights. As South African theologian Derek Morphew underscores:

"Human rights represent possibly the most pressing global issue of our time. The gravity of this issue alone compels thoughtful Christians to engage with it. At a deeper level, the fight for human rights touches on the essence of humanity, its potential, and destiny. Any thought or endeavor concerning humanity's core must be of interest to those committed to the gospel of Jesus Christ, as he came to seek and save this very humanity."

The brilliant giant of the Middle Ages, Thomas Aquinas, taught that both nature and government are subject to divine law. This philosophy has inspired many landmark human rights documents, including the

> There are clear Biblical instructions that Christians must take action to help the oppressed and the powerless. This is due to the Christians' responsibility, owed to God, to love their neighbors as themselves. This responsibility extends to upholding the rights of others and taking practical action to assist the oppressed and disadvantaged. This responsibility is, sadly, not widely understood either by Christians or by the Christian Churches.

American Declaration of Independence of 1776, which states: "we hold these truths to be self-evident: that all men are created equal, that they are endowed by their Creator with certain inalienable rights, that among these are life, liberty, and the pursuit of happiness."

Christian Churches as institutions are obligated to resist human rights violations whenever and wherever they occur. This resistance can take many forms such as issuing public statements, leveraging their moral authority in societies, and inspiring their congregations to take up the human rights cause. While the tension between God and earthly authorities merits a separate discussion, it's notable that both international human rights law and Christianity share common ground in rejecting absolute state power.

International human rights law places a primary responsibility on governments for protecting human rights. But it also urges all individuals to recognize and respect the rights of others, as exemplified by Article 29 of the Universal Declaration of Human Rights. Christians, however, bear a unique dual responsibility. They are obligated both horizontally to their fellow humans and vertically to God. God's demand that these rights be upheld is unequivocal. The parable of the Good Samaritan illustrates that our responsibility to others transcends causal relationships or familiar ties. No human is a stranger, and all Christians bear the divine duty to care for all. Acting to aid the oppressed is not just an act of charity, but a mandate for every Christian – a mandate that is answerable to God.

ACTUAL MESSAGE FROM PASTOR LORENZO R. FAJARDO

«LA ÚNICA COSA NECESARIA PARA EL TRIUNFO DEL MAL, ES QUE LOS HOMBRES BUENO NO HAGAN NADA» (EDMUN BURKE)

TEMA: EL CRISTIANO Y LA POLÍTICA
TEXTO: (DANIEL 6: 1-4) - (PROVERBIOS 3:8)
¡LEVANTA LA VOZ POR LOS QUE NO TIENEN VOZ!
¡DEFIENDE LOS DERECHOS DE LOS DESPOSEÍDOS!
(NUEVA VERSIÓN INTERNACIONAL)
¿PUEDE UN CRISTIANO DEDICARSE A LA POLÍTICA?
¿SON COMPATIBLES LOS IDEALES Y LA PRÁCTICA CRISTIANA CON LAS ACTIVIDADES DEL GOBIERNO POLÍTICO?

ES VERDAD QUE EL TEMA ES BIEN COMPLEJO, YA QUE TIENE MUCHAS ARISTAS, Y TRATAREMOS DE REFLEXIONAR EN EL MISMO. MIREMOS EL EJEMPLO INSPIRADOR DEL PROFETA DANIEL ¡QUE INTERESANTE! ¡QUE MARAVILLOSO! UN HOMBRE DE DIOS, QUE ESTÁ EN LA CIMA DEL PODER, AMBIENTE EN EL QUE GENERALMENTE LOS HOMBRES PIERDEN LA CABEZA, Y DEJAN SEDUCIRSE POR LOS LUJOS, LOS VICIOS, Y LAS PRESIONES DE TODO TIPO, ASÍ COMO POR LAS AMBICIONES EGOÍSTAS; A SU VEZ ES TAN INTACHABLE EN SU CONDUCTA QUE NI LOS PROPIOS ENEMIGO PUEDEN ENCONTRAR ALGUNA FALTA O VICIO MEDIANTE LOS CUALES PODER ACUSARLO.

PODRÍAMOS TAMBIÉN HABLAR DE JOSÉ EN EGIPTO, DE MOISÉS COMO GOBERNADOR DEL PUEBLO DE ISRAEL, TAMBIÉN DEL REY DAVID, DE SU HIJO SALOMÓN; HOY TENEMOS MUCHOS CREYENTES MODERNOS ES DECIR DE NUESTRO TIEMPO, QUE EJERCEN POSICIONES GUBERNAMENTALES. EN EL NUEVO TESTAMENTO, ENCONTRAMOS A JUAN EL BAUTISTA ¿QUE PREDICÓ JUAN EL BAUTISTA? LUCAS 3, 10-20)
V: 11 (EL QUE TIENE DOS TÚNICAS, DE AL QUE NO TIENE; Y EL QUE TIENE QUE COMER, HAGA LO MISMO).
V: 14 TAMBIÉN LE PREGUNTARON UNOS SOLDADOS, DICIENDO: Y NO HAGÁIS EXTORSIÓN A NADIE, NI CALUMNIÉIS; Y CONTENTAOS CON VUESTRO SALARIO.
V: 19 JUAN REPRENDE A HERODES, POR LAS MALDADES QUE EL HABÍA HECHO - (MARCOS 6: 20---)
V: 20 JUAN FUE ENCERRADO EN LA CÁRCEL
JESUCRISTO: (JESÚS ACUSA A ESCRIBAS Y A LOS FARISEOS.) (MATEO 83: 13-29)

PARA MUCHOS CRISTIANOS, PARECE HOY UTÓPICO EN EL MUNDO EN QUE VIVIMOS, PUES HAY TANTOS INTERESES ECONÓMICOS Y POLÍTICOS MEZCLADO QUE NO DA LA SENSACIÓN DE QUE NADIE PUEDE ACCEDER O PERMANECER EN EL PODER SIN CORROMPERSE O SIN SER "BASADO" DE EL PORQUE MOLESTA. PERO LO QUE QUIERO DESTACAR AQUÍ ES EL PRINCIPIO DE LO LEGÍTIMO DE LA ACTIVIDAD POLÍTICA PARA EL HIJO DE DIOS.
DE ALLÍ A QUE SEA REALIZABLE ES OTRO TEMA.
PERO, EN CASO DE QUE TE SIENTES LLAMADO A UNA VOCACIÓN POLÍTICA, O LA ESTÉS EJERCIENDO, RECUERDA QUE LA CLAVE PARA SEGUIR SIENDO CRISTIANO EN CUALQUIER POSICIÓN ES QUE COMO DANIEL, SEA FIEL HASTA LAS ÚLTIMAS, INTACHABLE, Y QUE LEJOS DE FORTALECER CON TU VIDA LA IDEA DE QUE "TODO HOMBRE TIENE SU PRECIO" Y PUEDA MOSTRAR QUE POR LA GRACIA DE DIOS, ERES INCOMPARABLE, Y QUE ESTÁS ALLÍ, SOLAMENTE PARA CONTRIBUIR AL BIENESTAR DE LA SOCIEDAD, Y NO PARA SATISFACER INTERESES PERSONALES EGOÍSTAS. Y MOSTRAR A UN DIOS JUSTO Y BUENO. AL REY DE REYES Y SEÑOR DE SEÑORES.

The protection of human rights by the international legal system is compatible with Christian teachings, despite some differences in emphasis. Rights and responsibilities are intrinsically connected. In fact, the active participation of Christians in the fight for human rights could potentially broaden the scope of responsibilities outlined in international human rights law. After all, 'what unites us as bearers of the image of God is more important than what divides us as members of nations.'

The Relationship Between Christians and Politics

The relationship between Christianity and politics has been a historically complex and contentious subject, leading to disagreements throughout the history of Christianity and even in modern politics, between the Christian right and the Christian left. Various thinkers have conceptualized this relationship in different ways, with some arguing that Christianity inherently supports a specific political ideology or philosophy, while others believe that Christians should distance themselves from politics and government.

Pope Francis addressed this issue in 2016 at the Vatican during the "Judges' Summit on Human Trafficking and Organized Crime." He emphasized that the Church must actively engage in the significant political issues of our time. Quoting Pope Paul VI, he highlighted that "political life is one of the highest forms of charity." The Pope further emphasized the Church's obligation to be faithful to the needs of the people, especially in times of deep suffering and ethical dilemmas, where faith, values, and social sciences converge.

Roberto Jesús Quiñones Haces, a Cuban lawyer, independent journalist, and Catholic who endured one year of imprisonment under horrifying conditions for defending his clients, expressed his view on the Church's role in politics during a human rights conference at Florida International University. He stated that the Church is not a political party but should not shy away from participating in the struggle for citizen improvements and standing up against injustices. For the Church to fulfill its calling, it must be a center for open exchange of ideas and debates that address the issues faced by its homeland and extend toward a greater social impact.

Biblical verses such as Romans 13:1 and 1 Peter 2:13-14 highlight the importance of submitting to governing authorities as they are established by God. However, it is crucial to note that God also holds these leaders accountable for the authority they wield. When leaders act unjustly, it is not a reflection of God's character, but rather the result of their own actions. Romans 13 makes it clear that leaders have the authority to lead their nations, but they must do so justly and righteously.

Participating in politics goes beyond simply casting votes during elections. Christians are called to be good stewards of their time on earth while acknowledging that their ultimate citizenship lies in heaven. This principle is exemplified in the words of the prophet Jeremiah, who urged God's people in exile to engage in society and work for the welfare of the city they inhabit. As the "salt of the earth" and the "light of the world," Christians are responsible for the flourishing of their world. Just as a single light can dispel darkness in a room, Christians must actively care for their culture and engage in the political processes of their society as part of their responsibility as God's people.

Voting is an essential aspect of political engagement, but it is only the starting point. Christians are called to participate actively in the political arena, advocating for justice, defending the oppressed, and seeking the welfare of their communities and nations. By doing so, they fulfill their role as agents of positive change and bearers of God's love and compassion in the world.

Section VI
Faith-Based Defiance: Acts of Resistance and Bravery

Embedding the timeless truth from the sacred scripture of Deuteronomy 31:6, "Be strong and courageous. Do not fear or be in dread of them, for it is the Lord your God who goes with you. He will not leave you or forsake you," renowned evangelist Billy Graham boldly advocated the necessity of moral courage to uphold Christian values in society. His words bear witness to the critical need to defend the virtues of justice, honor, and righteousness: "The Christian is to take his place in society with moral courage to stand up for that which is right, just, and honorable;" "Nowhere in the Bible does it teach that we are to withdraw ourselves from society. Rather, it teaches quite the contrary. We are to join with others who are working to good purpose to help lift the unfortunate."

Taking inspiration from Thomas Jefferson's conviction in his divine calling, as reflected in his powerful words, "Resistance to tyrants is obedience to God," we understand that succumbing to or serving such oppressors constitutes an act of defiance against the highest authority, the King of kings.

Underlining this viewpoint, four essential tenets of Christian civil disobedience are presented:

1. Christians should resist a government that mandates or fosters evil, striving nonviolently within the law to change a government that allows such actions.

2. Civil disobedience is warranted when the government's laws or orders blatantly contradict God's laws.

3. If a Christian disobeys an unjust government and cannot escape its jurisdiction, they should accept the government's retribution.

This chapter elucidates these tenets with biblical references and celebrates the defiance and courage displayed by various figures in history.

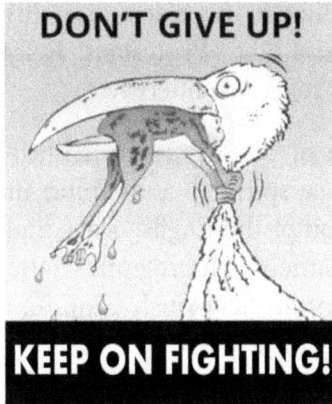

DON'T GIVE UP!

KEEP ON FIGHTING!

Civil Disobedience: Diverse Perspectives

Three prevailing perspectives frame the discourse on civil disobedience. The anarchist view promotes individualistic rebellion against the government, devoid of any biblical endorsement, as emphasized by Paul in Romans 13. The ultra-nationalist view proposes absolute adherence to one's country, irrespective of its commands—a stance lacking both biblical and historical validation. The third perspective, endorsed by the Scriptures, advocates biblical submission, permitting civil disobedience against a government enforcing evil actions contradictory to God's Word.

Christian involvement in civil disobedience signifies resistance against oppressive authorities, coupled with a readiness to bear the associated consequences.

Portraits of Courage and Resistance

A paramount exemplar of religious freedom's defense is Jan Hus, the 15th-century Czech theologian, philosopher, and reformer. He vehemently opposed the sale of indulgences, the Church's prevalent practice of selling absolution from sin. Further, he promoted preaching in vernacular languages over Latin, broadening the accessibility of religious services.

His potent advocacy for religious tolerance and the right to personal interpretation of the Bible signified a major stride for freedom of religion. Although his teachings antagonized the religious and political powers of his era, leading to his execution, his enduring influence became a cornerstone of the Protestant Reformation and future movements promoting religious liberty.

Another shining beacon of bravery is the British abolitionist William Wilberforce. Following a spiritual awakening in 1786, Wilberforce committed to the abolition of the English slave trade, braving vilification and roadblocks in Parliament. His relentless efforts eventually led to the eradication of slavery in the British Empire, marking a significant turning point in world history.

In the recent past, between 2019 and 2022, Catholic bishops and priests in Nicaragua stood as staunch defenders of freedom, challenging the oppressive reign of Ortega. During the 2018 protests against proposed pension reform, the Church opened its doors to the wounded and the medics, countering the government's repression.

God's Hand in Political Leadership

The Bible is replete with stories of political leaders chosen by God to advance His kingdom on earth. These accounts serve as guiding lights in the fight for religious freedom.

Foundational Biblical References on Civil Disobedience

Jesus Christ laid the cornerstone principle for balancing spiritual and secular responsibilities, as recorded in Matthew 22:21: "Render to Caesar the things that are Caesar's, and to God the things that are God's."

Peter's counsel provides further clarity: "Be subject for the Lord's sake to every human institution, whether it be to the emperor as supreme, or to governors as sent by him to punish those who do evil and to praise those who do good. . . . Honor everyone. Love the brotherhood. Fear

God. Honor the emperor" (1 Peter 2:13-14, 17).

In cases of conflict, we are called to obey our highest authority, God. However, this position should be taken only when necessary, first seeking every possible means to obey secular authorities while remaining true to the Lord.

The ordeal faced by Chinese Christians in 2017, who were coerced to replace Jesus's images with those of President Xi Jinping, or the believers in Cuba who faced adverse consequences unless they renounced their faith, are contemporary instances of such situations.

Even when political leaders must be opposed, it should be in the spirit of Christ. It is crucial to approach those with conflicting views respectfully and honestly, always "speaking the truth in love" (Ephesians 4:15). As ambassadors of Christ, we must remember our responsibility to reflect His character in all our actions and words.

Defiant Faith: Civil Disobedience in the Bible

Historically, religious faith has served as an unyielding fortress against tyranny and despotism. This section of the book pays tribute to the spirit of civil disobedience, as showcased by individuals who, motivated by their faith, stood defiantly against regimes that sought to suppress religious freedom. Their audacious acts of resistance are testament to the indomitable human spirit and a reminder that freedom of religion is a fundamental human right.

In the Biblical text of Exodus 1, two Hebrew midwives are commanded by the Egyptian Pharaoh to exterminate all male Jewish newborns. Despite the perilous consequences of defiance, the midwives chose to obey their faith over the commands of the state, thereby saving countless lives. Their disobedience was a courageous affirmation of the sanctity of life over the tyranny of man.

In the book of Joshua, Rahab directly defies the king of Jericho's orders to betray the Israelite spies, instead assisting in their escape. This act of resistance, not only saved the lives of the spies but also secured Rahab's own salvation during the subsequent destruction of Jericho by Joshua and the Israeli army.

In 1 Samuel, King Saul orders his own son Jonathan to death for disobeying a command issued during a military campaign. The people, however, rallied to Jonathan's defense, actively challenging and overturning the king's order—an act that embodied collective resistance against oppressive authority.

When the queen Jezebel commenced her brutal campaign against God's prophets, a man named Obadiah, deeply devout and God-fearing, sheltered a hundred prophets from her deadly wrath. His defiance in the face of royal edict, as recorded in 1 Kings 18, exemplifies a righteous rebellion rooted in faith.

In 2 Kings, the text narrates an approved revolt against a despotic ruler, Athaliah. She sought to annihilate the royal offspring of the house of Judah, threatening the sacred lineage. However, the young Joash was concealed from her, and six years later, a rebellion led by Jehoiada overthrew Athaliah and installed Joash as king, thereby preserving the holy lineage.

The Book of Daniel provides us with further instances of civil disobedience. Shadrach, Meshach, and Abednego refuse to bow down to King Nebuchadnezzar's golden idol. Later, Daniel himself defies King Darius' decree to pray only to the king. In both instances, their faith-led defiance not only thwarts the unjust edicts but also brings divine deliverance from the consequent death penalties.

Acts of the Apostles in the New Testament records Peter and John's civil disobedience against religious authorities. Following the miraculous healing of a man born lame, the apostles were prohibited from teaching about Jesus. Unbowed, Peter declared, "We must obey God rather than men" (Acts 5:29), expressing an unwavering commitment to their faith and freedom to express it.

The final act of civil disobedience is portrayed in the book of Revelation where the Antichrist demands the worship of his image. Those who convert to Christianity during this period, as prophesied by Apostle John, will reject this command, refusing to compromise their faith even under the shadow of the Antichrist.

The theme of faith-inspired defiance is evident in the story of Joseph who, sold into slavery, rises to become the prime minister of Egypt, and in the narratives of Israel's leaders like Moses, Joshua, and the Judges who guided their nation against oppressive forces. We see it in Mordecai, who stood resolute against Haman's plot to annihilate the Jews in Persia, and in Daniel and his companions who flourished in positions of political authority despite being exiles in Babylon.

All these instances illustrate the compelling power of faith to resist political coercion and protect religious freedom. This does not, however, eliminate the necessity of constructive dialogue and engagement with authority. As urged in 1 Timothy 2:1-2, Christians are to pray for their leaders, seeking divine intervention when leaders stray from the path of righteousness. A balance of faith-based defiance and spiritual intercession is key to promoting and preserving religious freedom.

SECTION VII
Championing Religious Liberty

"Speak out for those who are silenced, for the rights of all the marginalized. Advocate with fairness; defend the rights of the less fortunate and vulnerable." (Proverbs 31:8-9, NIV)

The fundamental human right of freedom of religion or belief (FoRB) is deeply embedded in Article 18 of the Universal Declaration of Rights (UDHR), as well as a multitude of international and regional human rights documents. This right, foundational to our human existence, explores the deepest commitments we pledge with our minds, hearts, and entire beings. Significantly, FoRB interconnects and interrelates with other fundamental rights like freedom of speech, assembly, and association. Violations of any of these rights often result in transgressions against others. Moreover, FoRB not only carries inherent value that makes its protection vital, but it also proves instrumental for the enjoyment of various public benefits, such as peaceful civic involvement and economic advancement.

Acknowledging its critical nature, my organization, OAA, has been defending religious freedom in Cuba for nearly three decades. We collaborate with local churches, church networks, and faith leaders to enhance their abilities as autonomous civil society contributors, human rights advocates, and humanitarian service organizations. OAA actively advocates for broader FoRB in Cuba, reports FoRB violations to the UN Special Rapporteur on Freedom of Religion or Belief (UNSR FoRB) and delivers training to faith leaders. OAA aligns with the UNSR FoRB's stance, who frequently calls attention to instances of religious persecution and violations in Cuba and Central America.

This section of the book collates a series of my opinion columns (Op-Eds) published in major outlets over the past decade, as well as testimonies delivered to U.S. Commissions on International

Religious Freedom. Each piece, some penned in Spanish, unravels complex themes and demonstrates my heartfelt and personal understanding of the significance of religious freedom.

These are my musings, derived from nearly thirty years of partnering with religious rights advocates in Cuba and Central America, experiencing life as a Christian, and championing their rights on an international stage. The articles encapsulate my intellectual worldview and my gratitude for the chance to experience life in liberty.

Contents

- (May 21, 2021)-Cuban Catholic Leaders Oppose Repression: They Need Our Support-The Miami Herald

- (July 27, 2021)-Cuban Religious Leaders' Preparedness for the Present Moment-The Sun Sentinel

- (October 5, 2021)-A Prayer for Cuba and Its People's Destiny-The Miami Herald

- (October 10, 2021)-Cuban Religious Leaders Unite for National Reform-El Nuevo Herald

- (March 29, 2022)-Religious Freedom Under Attack by Latin American Dictators Amid Focus on Ukraine-The Washington Examiner

- (September 1, 2022). "Pope Francis and His Concern for Nicaraguan Catholics". The Washington Examiner. Retrieved October 14, 2022.

- (December 8, 2022). "Justifying the US List Placement: Cuba and Nicaragua as Worst Violators of Religious Freedom". Miami Herald.

- (March 2, 2023). "Nicaraguan Bishop as a Symbol of Defiance to the Ortega Dictatorship". Miami Herald.

- (May 4, 2023). "What Catholic Bishops in Cuba Must Not Concede to the Regime". Miami Herald. Retrieved July 5, 2023.

- (June 28, 2023). Testimony to the U.S, Commission on International Religious Freedom (USCIRF)

- (July 5, 2023). "Highlight of Religious Freedom Week: The High Price Cubans Pay for Practicing Their Faith". Miami Herald. Retrieved July 5, 2023.

Posted at 01:22 PM ET, 03/26/2012 **The Washington Post**
How Pope Benedict could shape religious freedom in Cuba
By Teo A. Babun

Fourteen years ago, Pope John Paul II, a great champion of freedom and warrior against communism, visited the island of Cuba. And Monday, his successor, Pope Benedict XVI, will follow suit.

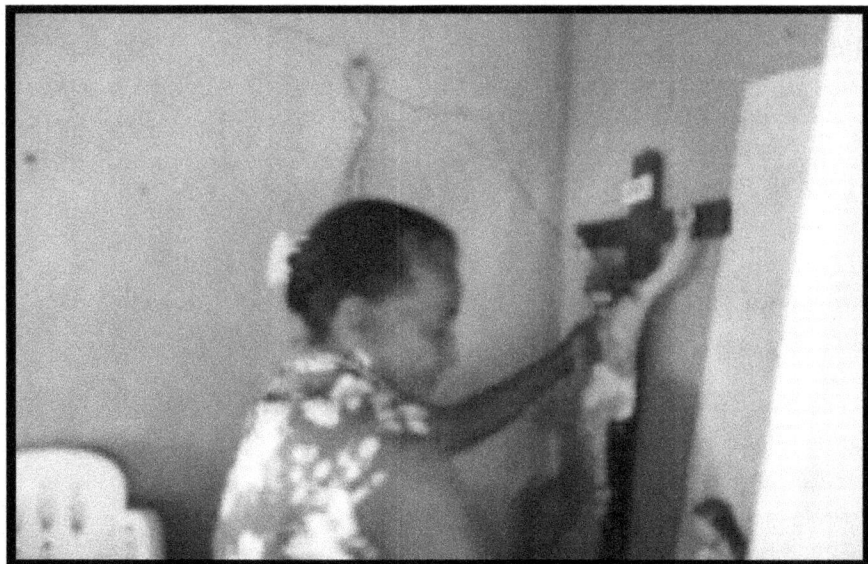

A parishioner attends a Catholic religious service held by Sister Cosafina with Mother Teresa's Missionaries of Charity at a poor rural mission house, or church, on the outskirts of Santiago called Juan Gonzalez on March 23, 2012 in Santiago de Cuba. Mission houses serve as churches in many rural parts of Cuba due to the lack of government sanctioned churches in the communist country. (Spencer Platt - GETTY IMAGES)

But this pope has the chance to avoid the political traps that diminished the political, if not the spiritual, impact of the visit of the last pope, and to carry on the legacy of his predecessor—who solidified the Catholic Church's position as the leader of the global cause for religious freedom.

Benedict's visit comes at a time when the Cuban government is amid an aggressive public relations campaign to present itself as reformist. Last December, the government announced it would be releasing nearly 3,000 prisoners in advance of the pope's visit. This notice came just a month after the government announced that for the first time since the communist revolution, the purchase and sale of private property would be legal.

Academics and diplomats around the world rejoiced and heralded a new era of change in Cuba. The Cuban exile community and those who know the oppressed nation more intimately knew better than to expect little more than a replay of 1998.

We remember the image of a fatigue-free and ex-communicated Castro greeting the pontiff in a crisp black suit. We recall his brother Raul smiling agreeably in the front rows of the papal Mass as the pope called for "true freedom" and "recognition of human rights and social justice." We recall a brief period of apparent change that former political prisoner Armando Valladares characterized as "cosmetic," at best.

In the words of Orlando Marquez, editor of Palabra Nueva, a publication of the Archdiocese of Havana, "It is as if those five days in January 1998 were an opened and closed parenthesis."

We recall that after he left, the dark curtain of oppression fell on the sunny island once more and religious oppression only escalated. In the decade and a half since his visit, thousands have been imprisoned in the Castro brothers' detention centers, and the government retains to this day a tight grip on religious freedom through the government-sanctioned Cuban Council of Churches

(CCC). Membership in the council is mandatory for the most rudimentary of rights, such as the right to hold a worship service or make basic repairs to a building, but most religious groups opt not to join, as compliance restricts religious practice just as severely.

From intra-Catholic perspective Pope John Paul II's trip was a success in planting seeds that have grown into what Miami Archbishop Thomas Wenski recently called a "springtime of faith," a revitalization of Catholic fervor especially notable among Cuban youth, as well as winning broader ground for the Catholic Church to practice more freely and openly without fear of reprisal.

But outside of Catholic circles, the visit fell short of making broader strides for religious freedom, largely because the Castro regime used the visit for an international aren't-we-actually-so-tolerant horse and pony show.

Benedict should take careful note of what his predecessor's visit taught us: Papal visits make for great opportunities for shammy public relations campaigns on the part of totalitarian governments.

But there is no reason Raul should get away with keeping the voices of non-Catholic religious leaders and their own faithful revivals and pleas for freedom from the ears of Pope Benedict as Fidel so artfully did with Pope John Paul II. Should the pope desire to make Cuba's oppressors squirm, he could:

- Meet with the Catholic youth groups in Santiago de Cuba who are advocating for freedom of religion through initiatives not funded by the official Catholic Church.

- Talk to the leaders of the independent evangelical churches, such as the eastern & western Baptists, Los Pinos Nuevos, or the Assemblies of God Conventions who represent most of the evangelical protestants in the island but are not allowed to be part of official visits because they are not members of the CCC, and

- Meet with the leaders of the non-government recognized (and therefore illegal) house church movement (Casas de Culto) and hear the grievances endured by the more than 35,000 house churches across Cuba.

While many of these figures do not look to the pope as a doctrinal shepherd, they view him as a shepherd of religious freedom, someone to hear their cries in the wilderness, an intercessor before the Cuban government and the world.

This pope has the opportunity to impact the island nation that has suffered under an atheist and totalitarian government for more than fifty years in that he comes at a time when his church is more vibrant and influential than ever. A Cuban Catholic community hungry for faith creates an energy the pope can channel toward demand for authentic religious freedom. But authenticity demands that the circle be widened beyond the Catholic community to include the marginalized, the de-legitimized, and the silenced. Because when the rights of one religious group are in jeopardy, the rights of all hangs in the balance.

The challenge Pope Benedict faces is how to turn a springtime of faith into a springtime of freedom.

Dr. Teo A. Babun, Jr. is the Executive Director of **ECHOcuba.**

The Miami Herald

In Cuba, religious freedom remains a dream.
Posted on Fri, Sep. 07, 2012
BY TEO A. BABUN JR.
Echocuba.org

BABUN JR.

Five nuns from Our Lady of the Good Shepherd's congregation returned to Cuba on Aug. 28 with a small statue they had taken 50 years ago when they left after Cuba's communist revolution. As recognition of the Cuban government's "advances" toward freedom of religion, the Episcopal Conference of Cuba noted that the religious act was "another sign of the improved relations between the church and the government."

Interestingly, this past summer, during remarks on the State Department's annual report on International Religious Freedom, Secretary of State Hillary Clinton said, "Freedom of religion is not just about religion." For Cubans, in particular, this is very true.

In Cuba, every aspect of life is controlled by the state. Freedoms in general — and specifically freedom of religion — are not fully available, and persecution of those who publicly profess a creed exists today. Freedom of religion is a right that every human being should be allowed to enjoy without restriction of any government or political entity.

Religion in Cuba must be presented in the context of its recent history, in a spirit of truth and justice, putting aside our personal interests or agendas — with no other objective except the truth.

When we talk about Cubans and religion, we must begin with what the people in Cuba have experienced and are experiencing today.

From the 1960s until 1990, discrimination against Christians slowed the growth of churches. Christians suffered under Cuban communism. In the early years some pastors and priests were placed in "re-education camps" a type of "concentration camp" where they were forced to perform manual labor in agriculture in order to survive — and where many met their death. These so-called camps were part of a rehabilitation program known as "military units to help agricultural production" or "UMAP" by its Cuban acronym.

Christians and their families could not receive a good education or good jobs. This pushed religious people to the lowest levels of society. Even by the mid-1980s, Cuba's government declared Christians could still not hold jobs where they would influence other people, especially children. This means no Christian teachers, social workers, counselors, etc. The result of these restrictions was that very few people wanted to be associated with Christianity as it would lead to the loss of job or status, as well as other discrimination.

One of the hardest realities of this strategy is that children are shamed by their teachers and others to disown religious symbols and renounce religious practices.

In his last newsletter published only a few weeks before his death, Oswaldo Payá, a Catholic, wrote that it is "shameful that a child must feel fear in her school because she attended a church service."

Religious leaders endure persecution and at times undergo threats from government officials. Some face difficult decisions when their lives and their families' lives are threatened. Due to fear, they comply with restrictions or requests to cease certain religious activity, such as outdoor concerts or baptism events.

Specific sectors of society, like the police and members of the military and their families, are still discouraged from participating in religious services. Lawyers, government workers and journalists are often effectively barred, usually under threat of losing their jobs.

Although officially the government does not favor any one church or religion, it appears to be more tolerant of those churches that maintain close relations with the state, such as those that belong to the "government friendly" Cuban Council of Churches.

It rewards them with special benefits (such as permits for outdoor services and youth camps). This exclusive favoritism is the cause for division with other religious institutions in the country.

The absence of religious freedom creates a climate of fear and lack of trust, which weakens civil society and creates greater distance between the citizens and those who govern them. And therefore, makes it more difficult to achieve any type of common national agenda.

Cubans should be free to promote the understanding of religious freedom embodied in the Universal Declaration of Human Rights (1948) and other international covenants to their fellow citizens.

Article 18 of the declaration states: "Everyone has the right to freedom of thought, conscience and religion; this includes freedom to change his religion or belief, and freedom, either alone or in community with others and in public or private, to manifest his religion or belief in teaching, practice, worship and observance."

The Cuban government has it wrong. These are human rights which provide dignity. It is the inherent patrimony of all human beings and a right of all Cubans. This is not something "allowed" or "gifted" by any country. Instead, it is the responsibility of governments to protect.

In Cuba, the church should be free to define the mission it believes it has received. Christians, Catholics, and other believers must be free to practice their faith in whatever manner they believe necessary. Unfortunately, this is not the case.

Teo A. Babun, Jr., is executive director of **ECHOcuba**, a Christian organization committed to helping support the independent church in Cuba.

© 2012 Miami Herald Media Company. All Rights Reserved.
http://www.miamiherald.com

𝕸iami 𝕳erald

Support Cubans who demand that freedom of religion be part of island's new constitution.

BY TEO BABUN
JANUARY 21, 2019, 05:45 PM,

Pastor Rafael Solano Silvera and his parishioners live in fear that the Cuban government will demolish their Familia Cristiana Baptist Church. Sadly, they're not alone. Across the island, religious leaders, their families and churches are reporting increased harassment that many see as a reaction to their demands for stronger protection of Freedom of Religion or Belief (FoRB) in the new constitution.

On Feb. 24, Cubans will vote Yes or No in a referendum for a new constitution, currently under public review. Its most recent draft eliminates references to freedom of conscience and significantly reduces protections for FoRB. Louise Tillotson, of Amnesty International, told Al Jazeera that the language "continues to be quite hazy and opens the door for criminal laws to be applied towards people that are deemed to be 'subversive'."

FoRB violations in Cuba have steadily increased over the past decade, with alarming spikes in recent years. Widespread repression and violence include church demolitions, harassment and detention of religious activists, and declaring more than 1,000 churches illegal. Buses serving churches involved in the constitutional referendum have been impounded, their drivers detained and threatened. Priests have been warned to abstain from commenting on the constitution.

As President and CEO of Outreach Aid to the Americas, (OAA), I have worked with my team and partners for more than two decades to strengthen the church in Cuba and empower citizens to affirm their basic human right to practice the religion or belief of their choice. In the face of increasing government manipulation to control and divide churches, we work to build the capacity and promote unity among church leadership.

Recently, church leaders have been shifting from maintaining their customary low profile to taking great risks to cast light on government efforts to weaken constitutional guarantees of freedom and conscience. Churches joined together to force transparency during a "constitution's consultative process," which presents a false front while intimidating people of faith. They have delivered two petitions to the Cuban government, one signed by more than 179,000 citizens. We support their brave efforts and call on all people of faith and conscience to stand behind them.

One of our partners, CSW, reports that the Cuban government continues to commit serious FoRB violations. Informants infiltrate and report on religious groups while a relentless, sometimes violent, campaign discourages members of independent civil society organizations from participating in religious activities.

CSW's report reinforces statements from the U.S. Commission on International Religious Freedom (USCIRF), as well as 30 individuals, religious groups, the Cuban Catholic Bishops Conference and Protestant leaders across the island. USCIRF's Kristina Arriaga has said: "The integrity of this historic process is in serious question if religious leaders are being ignored, then pressured to publicly support a new constitution that fails to protect their rights."

CSW Chief Executive Mervyn Thomas stresses that the current proposal that reduces protections for religious freedom is unacceptable. Both Arriaga and Thomas urge the Cuban government to immediately halt intimidation and fully consider citizens' input. Thomas calls on the international community "to push Cuba to ensure that its new constitution, including provisions on thought, conscience and religion, is fully in line with the Universal Declaration of Human Rights."

Citizens in the Americas — and around the world — should not let this crucial opportunity for substantive change in Cuba's constitution pass by. They can contact the U.S. Department of State and the White House to urge them to reach out to the

United Nations, European Union and Latin American countries with constructive influence with the Cuban government to show them that they are being watched, and to demand that this new wave of persecution ends.

All Cubans should have the basic human right to have a say in their new constitution and vote freely without undue pressure or manipulation. Help us ensure that Cuba's new constitution meaningfully addresses FoRB so that millions of Cuban citizens can breathe easy and practice their faith freely for generations to come.

Teo Babun is president and CEO of Outreach Aid to the Americas Inc., which is based in Miami.

The Miami Herald
MiamiHerald.com

OPINION

March 3, 2019
Cuba's new constitution fails to guarantee fundamental freedoms. Cubans saw through the charade.
BY TEO BABUN | @TEOBABUN

In the days before the so-called "national referendum" on revisions to Cuba's constitution, the Assemblies of God Pastor Robert Veliz Torres was arbitrarily detained for two hours by an agent from the Technical Department of Investigations (DTI). He was accused of directing members of his congregation to vote No.

Also, the president of the Western Baptist Convention received a call from Sonia García García, the deputy head of the Office of Religious Affairs, an arm of the Central Committee of the Cuban Communist Party, in which she said that, "From now on, Carlos Sebastián [the convention's general secretary] will no longer be treated as a

Pastor Mario Felix Lleonart being arrested in Cuba for his advocacy.

pastor, but as a counter-revolutionary." Sebastian's crime was that he told his church members that the new constitution lacked fundamental a "freedom of religion" language and for that reason he intended to No.

There were other reported arrests, intimidations and abuses leading up to the referendum. Government-produced billboards, posters and media messages urged citizens to vote Yes.

On Feb. 24, Cubans went to the polls to vote on a new constitution. The result, according to international press headlines, was that Cubans voted overwhelmingly for change, with 86 percent of voters approving the new constitution.

The truth, however, is that we don't know the real numbers. Like all elections in Cuba, there is no transparency and no observers from civil society or the international community. What we do know is that the government of Cuba drew a line in the sand and resorted to hard-nosed measures to ensure that advocates for a No vote were identified and threatened.

On Feb. 21, Madrid-based CubaData published the results of a poll showing widespread rejection of the regime's new constitution. The poll showed that 41.60 percent of Cubans were willing to vote No, and that 16 percent would abstain. CubaData's results were based on a sample of 1,000 Cubans from all over the country, polled from Feb. 16-18. The minimal difference between Yes voters (424) and No (416) constituted a technical tie only three days before the vote.

In response to the published results, U.S. Secretary of State Michael Pompeo said in an official statement that, "No one should be fooled by this exercise, which achieves little beyond perpetuating the pretext for the regime's one-party dictatorship". "The entire process has been marked by carefully managed political theater and repression of public debate."

He added that while the regime claimed that the vote was democratic, "Cuban authorities harassed and detained dozens of observers and peaceful protesters, confiscating phones and devices."

According to Christian Solidarity Worldwide (CSW), in the run-up to the vote, the government singled out potential opposition to the new constitution and ensured they knew they were being watched. What the Cuban government did not anticipate was two petitions drafted by religious leaders who objected to a constitutional article allowing same-sex marriage as well as constitutional language that diluted freedom of religion guarantees.

The same-sex marriage article was later dropped when 179,000 Cubans signed the petitions — an unprecedented show of dissent in authoritarian Communist Cuba. The Cuban Conference of Catholic Bishops followed with a strong public statement denouncing various articles of the new constitution while pointing out that it was not compatible with the church's moral, ethical, or civic values.

As the referendum approached, CSW reports, church pastors were detained, worshipers were threatened, and young church members were given pre-arrest warrants. Other dissenters who tried to vote were reportedly taunted and ridiculed by pro-government elements outside the polling stations.

As sad as this is, CSW's report describes it as a watershed moment: "The churches' reluctance to engage politically changed dramatically in the last eight months. For the first time, we saw religious leaders across the island working together, openly expressing their criticism of the constitution."

The Cuban government wants the world to believe that all Cubans are of one mind, committed to the Castros' socialist state. But we know better. Cubans suffer daily from the broken promises of a failed state, and there is a growing chorus of those that want legitimate, democratic reform.

Teo Babun is president and CEO of Outreach Aid to the Americas, Inc., also known as **EchoCuba.**

Miami Herald

Religious leaders in Cuba are bravely confronting the regime's oppression | Opinion

BY TEO BABUN

AUGUST 12, 2019 06:01 PM, UPDATED AUGUST 12, 2019 10:01 PM

Catholic leaders in Cuba were prohibited from attending the funeral of Cardinal Jaime Ortega y Alamino, the archbishop of Havana who died in July at 82.

Despite claims that it respects freedom of religion and belief, the Cuban government views religious advocates as problematic "counter-revolutionaries." Through its Office of Religious Affairs — the main perpetrator of religious repression in Cuba — the government treats religious activists like common criminals. It divides the faith community by including a few in its tightly controlled Cuba Council of Churches, while treating others as troublemakers.

Last year, Catholic and Protestant religious leaders and followers called for stronger protections for freedom of religion and freedom of conscience to be included in the new constitution before it went to public referendum. Church leaders bravely united to expose the Cuban government's efforts to water down previous constitutional guarantees of freedom by initiating two petitions, one signed by 180,000 Cuban citizens.

The Cuban government is retaliating. Last week, the Office of Religious Affairs canceled the National Catholic Youth Day, even though all permits were granted. Catholic priest Jorge Luis Perez said the arbitrary cancellation affected more than 3,000 young people's spiritual retreat.

In addition, the regime prohibited Catholic lay leaders from attending funeral services for Cardinal Jaime Ortega y Alamino, who died last month. And some of the largest Protestant denominations, including the Methodist Church, the Evangelical League and the Eastern Baptist Convention, reported that they are banned from receiving foreign visitors in apparent retaliation for the formation of an independent Cuban Evangelical Alliance.

Last April, Rev. Ramon Rigal and his wife, Ayda Expósito, were jailed because they refused to send their children to government-run schools. The family, members of the Church of God, was given 30 minutes' notice before their trial began, thus denying them legal representation. Their children have been studying through an accredited international homeschooling program given the parents' concern about how the regime indoctrinates young Cubans in socialism and atheism. Christian Solidarity Worldwide reports other such cases in Cuba. Numerous religious groups, including the Catholic Church, have repeatedly advocated for reform, to no avail.

Last month, Cuban government officials told the heads of five evangelical denominations that they were prohibited from leaving the island to attend the second annual international Ministerial to Advance Religious Freedom in Washington, which more than 1,000 religious advocates from

110 countries attended. The five pastors are founders of the Cuban Evangelical Alliance. Another leader, the president of the Baptist Convention of Cuba, was also blocked from attending.

The government's action followed the arbitrary detention of religious freedom defender Ricardo Fernandez Izaguirre on July 12. He was held in a small cell, incommunicado and without access to medicines, before being released a week later. for 30 days. He never was told why.

Advocates for freedom are reacting. Kimberly Breier, undersecretary of State for Western Hemisphere Affairs, criticized the Cuban regime, asking, "Why does the [Cuban government] prevent religious leaders from attending? The people of Cuba will never reach their potential under a government that does not respect fundamental freedoms and restricts the movement of religious leaders and other courageous defenders of human rights."

Secretary of State Michael R. Pompeo lamented the "thuggish, intolerant nature of the current regime in Havana." Through the Office of Religious Affairs, the government is increasing threats, travel restrictions, detentions and violence against religious leaders and followers, even restricting the rights of prisoners to worship. The government harasses and detains people advocating for religious and political freedom, including the well-known Ladies in White, who are not allowed to attend Catholic Mass.

Freedom of religion is intrinsic to social good and, like freedom of expression and assembly, is central to the Universal Declaration on Human Rights. But these essential liberties, as well as the development of a truly independent civil society, are restricted by a government that fears upheaval, legitimate reform and loss of power.

This is a watershed moment. Despite harsh and inevitable government reprisal, independent church leaders have emerged as Cuba's most powerful — and respected — civil-society activists for freedom of religion and belief and the intersectional rights of expression, assembly, association, education, nondiscrimination, privacy and due process. This is the time to support efforts both on the island and internationally for engagement, advocacy, and action on fundamental liberties in Cuba.

Teo Babun is president and CEO of Outreach Aid to the Americas, Inc., also known as EchoCuba.

U.N. unleashes new ally in fight against religious repression in Cuba -The Miami Herald - OPINION

BY TEO BABUN
NOVEMBER 14, 2019 6:18 PM

As the United Nations Special Rapporteur for Cuba, Ahmed Shaheed is monitoring religious repression on the island. Office of the United Nations High Commissioner for Human Rights. Ahmed Shaheed, the United Nations Special Rapporteur (UNSR) for Cuba, reports that current laws in Cuba allow the government to prohibit and penalize a broad range of protected religious activities. Large-scale detentions increased in 2016 and 2017, and the government even detained the entire congregation of the Emanuel Apostolic Church in Santiago, destroying their building and confiscating church property.

Shaheed's report marks a promising shift. Though Cuba is widely acknowledged to be the Western Hemisphere's worst abuser of fundamental freedoms, until recently the United Nations, including past UNSRs entrusted with monitoring and reporting on freedom of religion and belief worldwide, has paid scant attention to deplorable repression on the island.

For years, U.N. human-rights accountability mechanisms routinely have failed to flag widespread, systematic, and well-documented repression of churches, congregations, religious leaders, and worshipers by the Cuban government.

Shaheed previously served five years as UNSR for human rights in

Iran. He now is broadening his office's focus to Cuba for the first time. A highly respected academic and senior government official, he has the well- earned reputation as a tough, fair-minded advocate for individuals who demand the freedom to practice the religion they choose. At long last, the U.N. is deepening its engagement with global religious communities that grapple with poorly understood challenges to their right to religious freedom. My organization, EchoCuba, is encouraged to see a man such as Shaheed in this crucial role.

Like many Communist governments, the Cuban government uses a defensive playbook to stymie anyone who strives to expose its numerous human-rights abuses. It maintains that critics of its harsh treatment of "counterrevolutionaries" — people who express political opinions that don't follow Socialist dogma, groups that practice faiths of which the government disapproves — are just patsies under a U.S.-led campaign aimed to support regime change.

Indeed, Cuba always maintains that it is unfairly targeted. Shaheed knows otherwise. In his 2019 report, he observes that Cuba's penal code allows imprisonment of people whose religious beliefs conflict with the nation's Socialist principles related to education, labor, defense, and reverence of symbols. From our work in Cuba for more than 25 years, we welcome Shaheed's findings, still knowing they provide only an initial rough sketch of rampant abuses that continue today.

Dedicated organizations such as Christian Solidarity Worldwide (CSW) are reporting an uptick in repressive government practices that violate freedom of belief around the world. As recently as July and August, CSW documented several cases of arbitrary detentions, church property confiscation, harassment, threats, worshippers prevented from attending church services, religious leaders blocked from traveling abroad and religious events that were forced to cancel.

CSW and other international observers have identified a large number of Cubans languishing in the government's vast prison population, punished for purely political and/or religious reasons. Cuba's religious freedom regulator, the Office of Religious Affairs, its prosecutors, and police, use extra-legal, opaque administrative rules and procedures to target and punish Cubans who have the courage to exercise their right to freedom of religion and to associate with churches the government does not sanction.

Shaheed has requested that the Cuban government approve an official fact-finding visit to the island next year. We know he will bring the same integrity and tenacity to Cuba that he has to other parts of the world. We trust he will expand his review of religious repression, documented daily by Cuba's dedicated defenders, and engage directly with the government to eliminate religious repression.

It is long past time for all UNHRC members to call out Cuba — ironically a UNHRC member itself — on its atrocious behavior. Continued failure to do so would undermine the integrity of what should be the world's premier human-rights council and betray ordinary Cubans who simply want to practice the faith of their choice.

*Teo Babun is president and CEO of Outreach Aid to the Americas, Inc., also known as **EchoCuba**.*

el Nuevo Herald

Cuba viola el derecho a la libertad de religión y circulación
POR TEO BABUN ACTUALIZADO 15 DE NOVIEMBRE DE 2019 2:48 PM

JONATHAN BUTTLE-SMITH Unsplash

El gobierno de Cuba viola la libertad de religión y circulación ante los ojos del mundo. Una prueba más está en la prohibición de salida del país a una veintena de líderes y/o activistas religiosos sin una causa explícita.

La más reciente violación fue contra Josué Rodríguez Legrá, presidente de la Convención Bautista de Cuba Oriental, en Santiago de Cuba. Estaba invitado a un evento religioso en la Florida, pero en el aeropuerto le dijeron que no podía salir y que "él sabría por qué".

La Convención Bautista de Cuba Oriental se sumó a una Alianza de Iglesias Evangélicas Cubanas que responde, según declaran, a una expresión de unidad entre cristianos. Pero el gobierno la asume como una amenaza.

Las prohibiciones de viajes al exterior son un castigo que imponen a opositores, periodistas independientes, activistas por los derechos humanos y a cuantos representen un pensamiento libre. Los líderes y activistas religiosos forman parte de este último grupo. Por eso, a más de 20 de ellos se les ha aplicado el término de "regulados"; una etiqueta que utilizan las autoridades para violar, en este caso, la libertad de circulación, derecho recogido en el artículo 13 de la Declaración Universal de Derechos Humanos, de la que Cuba es signataria.

La paranoia revivió con la muerte de Fidel Castro. Por solo citar algunos casos, podemos recordar que el gobierno detuvo a toda la congregación de la Iglesia Apostólica Emanuel, en Santiago de Cuba, destruyendo luego el edificio y confiscando sus propiedades. En prisión permanece un matrimonio de pastores por intentar educar a sus hijos de acuerdo con sus principios. Encarcelado permanece un abogado, periodista independiente y laico católico por intentar cubrir el juicio de dicho matrimonio. ¿Cuánto más tiene que hacer La Habana en contra de la libertad para que el mundo reaccione ante los abusos a que son sometidos los verdaderos representantes de la sociedad civil cuba?

Organizaciones como el Instituto Patmos y Christian Solidarity Worldwidane (CSW) han documentado, entre julio y agosto de 2019, numerosos casos de detenciones arbitrarias, confiscación de bienes de la iglesia, hostigamiento, limitaciones de asistir a servicios religiosos, amenazas, difamaciones, cancelación de eventos y las mencionadas limitaciones de salida del país. CSW y otros observadores han identificado además a muchos cubanos que languidecen dentro de la vasta población carcelaria de Cuba, castigados por motivos políticos y/o religiosos.

Por más de 30 años, los informes anuales sobre libertad de religión o de creencias han mostrado a los estados miembros del Consejo de Derechos Humanos (CDH) de la ONU los atropellos a la libertad religiosa en países autoritarios como China o Irán, que colocan al estado por encima de los derechos y creencias individuales. Sin embargo, la represión enquistada, bien documentada y reportada que el gobierno cubano ejerce sobre iglesias, congregaciones, líderes religiosos y creyentes que defienden su libertad de conciencia ha conseguido pasar por alto. El 2019 debería marcar un nuevo rumbo.

En el último "Informe del Relator Especial sobre libertad de religión o creencias" de la ONU, se reconoce como el código penal de Cuba permite el encarcelamiento de aquellos cuyas creencias religiosas entren en conflicto con la ideología socialista en cuanto a la educación, el trabajo, la defensa y la reverencia a los símbolos. Desde nuestra labor en Cuba durante más de 25 años abogando por la libertad religiosa, nos alegra darles la bienvenida a estos "hallazgos" iniciales que constituyen una borrosa y aún incipiente instantánea de los atropellos castrenses a ciudadanos que tratan de ejercer su derecho a la libertad de religión y creencias.

Aunque el último informe sobre libertad de religión y creencias presentado a la CDH es un paso de avance hacia la sensibilización de la ONU, se necesita ampliar la revisión de los casos que documentan habitualmente los arriesgados defensores de los derechos religiosos en la isla y comprometer a las autoridades para eliminar la represión. El Relator Especial de las Naciones Unidas para Libertad de Religión o Creencia, Ahmed Shaheed, ha solicitado que el gobierno apruebe una visita oficial de investigación a la isla el próximo año. Esperamos que alcance a verla por dentro.

El gobierno cubano continúa con su vieja retórica de que todos los que atacan sus arbitrariedades y tratos severos son considerados nada menos que "contrarrevolucionarios", un saco grande donde caben los practicantes de creencias que las autoridades desaprueban, o cualquiera que resuene en paralelo a su experimento político. Es hora ya de que las Naciones Unidas empiecen a distinguir dónde termina la ficción y comienza la realidad de la represión en Cuba. Ignorar o atender a la ligera estos reclamos socavan la integridad de lo que debería ser el principal consejo de derechos humanos del mundo.

El Dr. Teo Babun es el Presidente y CEO de ECHOCUBA/Outreach Aid to the Americas, Inc. (OAA). La organización responde a las necesidades de las personas vulnerables, promueve el espíritu empresarial, las habilidades organizativas, educación, libertades religiosas y servicios sociales en Cuba y en la Región de las Américas.

The Miami Herald

Cuba stepped up its persecution of people of faith. Will it get worse in 2020? | Opinion

BY TEO BABUN
JANUARY 22, 2020, 7:16 PM

In Cuba last month, a gang of students severely beat a 12-year-old Jewish schoolboy. The school guard had prohibited the boy and his younger brother from entering the building. The two boys later were told that they would be allowed to attend class, but they were forbidden from wearing the kippah, their traditional Jewish head covering.

When the boys' parents sought justice, they were threatened.

Christian Solidarity Worldwide (CSW) has documented many cases where children of different faiths in Cuba were singled out or denied an education in 2019. Their parents often were branded "counterrevolutionaries." Pastor Ramon Rigal and his wife, Ayda Expósito, currently are imprisoned in eastern Cuba because they turned to homeschooling when their children were targeted for bullying and assault at a government-run school.

CSW's head of advocacy, Anna-Lee Stangl, says these cases illustrate "a more general hostility to religion within the Cuban school system."

She says that the past year has seen "new and worrying forms" in the ongoing decline of religious freedom. Cubans routinely are denied basic freedoms outlined in Article 18 of the Universal Declaration of Human Rights, e.g. openly sharing faith with others, giving children a formal and religious education, ministering in prisons and hospitals, accessing radio, TV and the internet. Over the past several years, pastors have been arrested, laptops and literature confiscated, churches shut down and demolished.

Catholic priest Castor José Álvarez Devesa laments that his country is "living in lies" and suppressing basic freedoms: "I was not allowed to conduct a procession of the Virgin through the bay of Nuevitas, using the seaway . . . not allowed, as a church, to open new houses of worship." When religious leaders like Castor address repression, when they call for unity and resistance, the harassment intensifies. Many are prevented from leaving Cuba.

And the propaganda never stops. Raul Castro's daughter Mariela accused Cuban evangelical leaders of receiving funding from the CIA. Similarly, as the head of a long-established nonprofit advocating for basic human rights on the island, I was fallaciously branded a mercenary for "sowing discord and charming religious leaders with the lure of humanitarian help."

The United States has denounced harassment of members of religious groups that advocate for religious and political freedom, including the much-respected Ladies in White. In December, Cuba was added to the State Department's special watch list of nations that violate religious freedom and reaffirmed the administration's commitment to promote freedom of religion and oppose abuses.

The Cuban government projects a facade of justice and religious freedom while it capriciously shifts tactics and employs covert approaches to discourage, frighten, intimidate and punish people of faith who seek to gather, worship, educate and unite.

Yet even in the face of these pressures, many Cubans fight on. A Catholic priest openly accuses the government of promulgating a "mentality of oppression." A group of young advocates posts a video detailing how the government manipulates Cuban citizens by allowing some religious space while denying other basic rights (https://www.youtube.com/watch?v=_BoU-g9q5t0).

To strengthen control over civil society, the Cuban government often portrays young people as apathetic. But this video contradicts that lie. A new generation of intelligent, focused activists is arising on the island. As Camilo Venegas, a leading Cuban writer, observes, "A young and deep Cuba has taken the torch of the struggle for civil rights and has the wonderful ability to convey its message. That will not be an isolated cry."

Will 2020 bring more religious repression? If we look the other way, it will. Support the people of Cuba through organizations such as Rights Watch and Christian Solidarity Worldwide. Communicate with elected representatives. Respond vigorously to violations of basic freedoms.

Share articles, blogs and videos. Stand with those who have the wisdom and courage to demand full freedom of religion on their island nation.

*Teo Babun is president and CEO of Outreach Aid to the Americas, Inc., also known as **EchoCuba**.*

𝕸iami 𝕳erald

Cuba uses the coronavirus crisis to continue to harass, imprison religious leaders | Opinion.
BY TEO BABUN
MAY 27, 2020 06:30 PM

To prevent hoarding during the pandemic, a soldier in Havana, Cuba, patrols outside a government-run food store where shoppers wait in line. RAMON ESPINOSA AP.

In early March, responsible governments around the world closed borders to protect public health. But not Cuba. Instead, the cash-strapped government proclaimed: Visit Cuba for a safe vacation! By late March, officials reported a rise in COVID-19 infections, predominantly among Italian and Spanish tourists.

The government currently reports 1,900 cases, but Cuba's Institute of Tropical Medicine counted almost half a million cases of acute respiratory illness from March 15 to April 4 — most presumably COVID-19.

This is an especially vulnerable time for Cuba. Prior to the pandemic, Cuba was experiencing a foreign-exchange crisis, coupled with chronic shortages of food, fuel, medicine and hygiene supplies; inadequate, overcrowded housing; weak medical infrastructure and insufficient healthcare workers; and growing discontent with leaders' lavish lifestyles while people wait in long lines for scarce food and soap.

Totalitarian governments such as China, Venezuela, Nicaragua and Cuba follow a common playbook: They are underreporting infections and deaths, expanding invasive surveillance, hoarding medical resources, and quickly disposing of victims through mass burials and cremations. They are further eroding basic rights by taking advantage of a distracted international community and exploiting fear, grief and chaos.

Erik Jennische, of Civil Rights Defenders, says that 96 percent of Cubans surveyed are reporting an increase in human-rights violations during the pandemic. State security agents accused the evangelical independent journalist Yoe Suárez of "dissidence" and "disseminating enemy propaganda." Suárez has been harassed four times so far during the lockdown, interrogated and threatened with imprisonment and repercussions for his family.

In these times, detention can be a death sentence. Religious leaders and other good Samaritans are being jailed simply for assisting elders and providing mutual aid to neighbors. Apostolic leader Yilber Durand Domínguez and Christian artist José Acebo Hidalgo were detained when they resisted letting government officials into their homes during quarantine — an unnecessary risk for their families. Domínguez was held in a large facility, and Acebo, who is visually impaired, faces prison for "disobedience" and other spurious charges.

Alaín Toledano, a church leader and regular government target, was detained and charged with "spreading epidemics" and "illicit enrichment" ostensibly related to church activities. Yoel Demetrio, president of the Missionary Church of Cuba, was arbitrarily confined in an overcrowded prison for two days.

The regime routinely prohibits evangelical leaders from broadcasting on TV and radio. Christian lawyer and activist Miguel Porres, featured in Cubadentro videos on Freedom of Religious Belief (FoRB), was detained and interrogated for two hours. In April, authorities betrayed the Evangelical Alliance by granting them the "privilege" of addressing the entire nation for Holy Week, then censoring their videos. National television broadcast a meeting of the Cuban Council of Churches (CCC), an institution many evangelicals do not trust because it answers directly to the Office of Religious Affairs (ORA). The faith community expressed discontent via social media.

The Cuban regime is weaponizing human suffering to escalate its regional power and destabilization efforts. Courageous Cubans who dare criticize the government are systematically deprived of their livelihoods and access to food and medicine. Such tactics lead to extreme levels of food insecurity and social disenfranchisement designed to silence advocates for justice and human rights.

This is a time of deep sadness. We are turning inward and asking how we can best take care of our neighbors, both on our street and on our planet. We must commit to refusing to turn a blind eye to repression worldwide, to calling out lies, cruelty and exploitation. We must stand with our brothers and sisters in Cuba and support them as they continue to affirm their basic human rights to freedom of thought, conscience, and religion.

Teo Babun is president and CEO of Outreach Aid to the Americas, Inc., also known as EchoCuba.

Link to Op-ed: https://www.miamiherald.com/opinion/op-ed/article243037981.html

Washington Examiner

November 5, 2020

Cuba should look to the former Soviet republic of Uzbekistan as an example for improving religious freedom.

For too long Cuba's authoritarian leaders have largely been able to avoid being held accountable for their numerous human rights abuses. Look no further than Cuba's election on October 13 to the UN Human Rights Council, where it will join other rights violators such as China and Russia, for a recent example. Still, this avoidance is becoming increasingly more difficult on the issue of religious freedom.

This year, the Cuban government's egregious and often violent disregard for this right caught the attention of human rights officials at the United Nations. On May 13, four Special Rapporteurs—on freedom of religion or belief, freedom of opinion and expression, freedom of peaceful assembly and of association, and minority issues—in addition to the working group on arbitrary detention, issued a communication to the Cuban government raising concerns about violations against a Cuban pastor and his church. According to the communication, since 2005, Cuban authorities have waged a "constant campaign of harassment and intimidation" against the pastor, Alain Toledano, his family, and the members of his Apostolic Movement church. Among other violations, authorities have prohibited the pastor from traveling outside of Cuba, and they have destroyed his church and seized its assets.

In his March 2019 report to the UN Human Rights Council, Ahmed Shaheed, the UN Special Rapporteur on freedom of religion or belief, offered Cuban authorities' treatment of Pastor Toledano and his church as an example of the Cuban government criminalizing religious beliefs that it considers to be in "conflict with the aims of education, the duties of labor, defending the nation in arms, the reverence of its symbols or any other stipulations whatsoever contained in the Constitution." (Needless to say, Cuba rejected this allegation.) Incidentally, in December 2018, the Special Rapporteur followed up on a 2006 request by his predecessor to visit the country to explore the situation of freedom of religion or belief in the country. However, to date, the government has remained silent on this new appeal.

Many governments view these country visits with suspicion and derision, often claiming that Special Rapporteurs are in the business of naming and shaming, rather than being honest brokers for promoting human rights. However, others view these visits as opportunities to identify issues of concern being monitored and documented by civil society, showcase their best practices and lessons learned, and to establish an ongoing dialogue with the international community and the UN human rights system in order to demonstrate their commitment to human rights and cooperation.

The Cuban government would do well to take the latter approach, and it can look to Uzbekistan as an example. Despite their many differences, there are several similarities between Cuba and Uzbekistan's treatment of religion. To name only two: in recent decades, both states somewhat relaxed their posture toward religion from one of ideologically based hostility to cautious tolerance, and both states view religious organizations as competitors and potential threats to government control.

However, in the last two to three years, Uzbekistan has taken some noteworthy steps demonstrating its commitment to improve religious freedom conditions. In 2017, Uzbekistan extended invitations to the UN High Commissioner for Human Rights and Mr. Shaheed to visit the country (it would be the Commissioner's first visit). In his report on his visit, Mr. Shaheed commended Uzbekistan for "full cooperation extended to him," for accommodating "all his requests for meetings," and "granting him unimpeded access to various institutions," including the infamous Jaslyk Prison, which is known by many as the "house of torture."

Among other recent reforms, Uzbekistan approved a bill to implement all 12 of the recommendations made by Mr. Shaheed. For these efforts, in 2018 the State Department rewarded Uzbekistan by taking it off its list of the world's worst violators of religious freedom, on which Uzbekistan had been since 2006. And although concerns remain,

Uzbekistan's leaders seem genuinely to want to make progress in this area.

Cuba's leaders should see the current work of the Special Rapporteur on freedom of religion or belief as an opportunity to engage constructively and make progress on this issue. For one, Cuba can take such steps, such as announcing that it will allow the Special Rapporteur to visit, as a kind of good-faith response to its recent election to the UN Human Rights Council, although it does not deserve a seat on this body. Of course, taking steps to guarantee religious freedom is the right thing to do for its own sake; but at least for the sake of improving its image on the world stage, the Cuban government can do a lot worse than to follow the example of Uzbekistan.

Dr. Teo Babún is the President and CEO of Outreach Aid to the Americas, a Miami-based nonprofit organization dedicated to serving vulnerable peoples in Central America and the Caribbean through humanitarian assistance, development efforts, and human rights advocacy.

OP-ED

The Miami Herald May 21, 2021
Catholic leaders in Cuba speak out against repression. They need our support.

As in most other places around the world, the Catholic clergy in Cuba are usually busy presiding over rituals and practices and instructing followers in the faith.

Parish priests celebrate daily Mass, hear confessions every week, visit the sick in hospitals and nursing homes, and offer spiritual direction. Nuns serve their community mostly through helping the poor, teaching after school, and providing health care. Committed to a life of faith, poverty, and chastity, they almost never get involved in the political or economic dialogue of the nation.

But a couple of weeks ago, something unusual happened. Eighteen Catholic orders who work in Cuba published an open letter to government authorities denouncing the lack of freedom of expression and the economic precariousness to which the island's population is subjected. It is no accident that the letter was circulated only days after a group of Catholic priests and lay ministers posted a video on social media demanding change and expressing support for a group of dissidents who went on hunger strike to call attention to repressive and brutal practices of the Cuban government.

There seems to be a gathering of momentum to the Catholic clergy's messages. For instance, in January, a virtual Catholic group named "Areópago Cubano" also published its own open letter titled, "I Have Seen the Affliction of My People", which details the suffering that the Cuban people are experiencing and calls for political change. To date, more than 1,000 people representing a variety of faiths and sectors in Cuba have signed the letter.

In the Areópago letter, crafted by 20 or so young priests from the province of Camagüey in the north central part of the island, the priests affirm that in Cuba, "the people have to learn to live in a 'desert of freedoms' where they must choose between freedom and the comforts of life." As impassioned and strongly worded as the priests' letters and statements are, their tone is always respectful and marked by love for country. In one instance, for example, the authors write that they "contemplate the reality of the Island with immense love, as a son does with his mother."

Faith workers such as these priests and nuns have the pulse of the people and the local communities. A large majority of Cubans profess religious faith, and as many as 70 percent identify with a specific church. Despite numerous and formidable government-imposed obstacles, church networks offer the largest and most viable civil society platforms for supporting development and humanitarian relief efforts.

The U.S Department of State agrees with the message of these Catholic leaders. Its 2020 Report on International Religious Freedom, released on May 12, states that "Catholic and Protestant Church leaders, both in and outside the government- recognized Council of Cuban Churches (CCC), continued to report frequent visits from state security agents and CCP officials for the purpose of intimidating them and reminding them they were under close surveillance." The report adds that Cuban Christians are prohibited from establishing schools, creating newspapers, or spreading their message through the media. Last December, the Secretary of State again placed Cuba on the Special Watch List for countries whose governments "engage in or tolerate" severe violations of religious freedom.

Recently, Cuban television and bloggers are trying to discredit the religious messengers by broadcasting their names and insinuating sexual and other kinds of misconduct. They have also slandered them by calling them mercenaries and terrorists. The organization I lead, Outreach Aid to the Americas (OAA), and others have urged the authorities to treat the religious advocates with dignity and respect.

There is no question that the regime's attacks are born out of its inability to control its critics or to refute criticisms of the island's grim realities — something that is plain to any honest observer of the reality on the island. Fundamentally, this is a government whose determination to cling on to power renders it unable to have a constructive dialogue with its citizens.

At OAA we advocate for freedom of thought, conscience and religion or belief as an essential human right without which there cannot be a healthy civic space. The time has come for the Cuban government to allow the faith community the freedom to exercise its calling to alleviate suffering and save lives.

Furthermore, when religious communities in Cuba face violations to freedom of religion or belief, other fundamental rights, such as freedom of expression, association, assembly, and movement, and the right to non-discrimination, are often curtailed as well. In denying these rights, the Cuban government is choking off the nation's nascent civil society, whose beauty, creativity, and initiative show us what a truly free Cuba can achieve.

Cuba's nuns, priests, pastors, and other faith leaders are respected voices in the community, and they are increasingly acting as brave human rights defenders who speak truth to power. The United States should work with international and regional stakeholders to generate external pressure while also fostering internal conditions that enable and protect civic space and human rights advocates, including faith-based actors, through a framework that links civic space to key aspects of the right to freedom of religion and belief.

SPECIAL TO THE SUN SENTINEL

Cuban religious leaders have been preparing for this moment | Opinion

By TEO BABUN

JULY 27, 2021 AT 8:00 AM

People take part in a demonstration against the government of Cuban President Miguel Diaz-Canel in Havana, on July 11, 2021. (ADALBERTO ROQUE/AFP/TNS)

On July 11, thousands of people from all over Cuba took to the streets to protest the communist leaders' failure to address economic, social and public health crises, and their continued, brutal authoritarian rule in a show of popular force not seen in decades. Despite the regime's unsurprisingly violent response, demonstrators continue to boldly pour out into the streets. You might say that the priests saw this coming.

Since last year, numerous Catholic priests and lay leaders, as well as some Protestant pastors, have been publicly making strong criticisms of Cuba's communist leaders not only for their continued human rights abuses but also for their incompetence and apparent callousness in the face of widespread suffering resulting from the pandemic and an economy in free fall. In homilies, sermons, open letters and social media posts, religious leaders expressed support for human rights advocates and called on the Cuban people to hold onto faith and hope at a time of severe national testing.

It is not incidental, then, that among those who were arbitrarily detained during the protests is Father Castor José Alvarez Devesa, a brave priest who has called for political change. Father Castor was severely beaten and held incommunicado before being released a day later. Other religious leaders who have been arrested are Baptist pastors Yarian Sierra, Yéremi Blanco, and Yusniel Pérez Montejo, who has since been released. The families of pastors Sierra and Blanco have been prevented from communicating with them.

It is likely that the regime saw in these events an opportunity to remove those whose outspokenness have made them a real threat to the survival of the regime. There are many other tools and tactics that the regime uses against religious leaders who refuse to "stay out of politics," as they are often warned to do. Many, for example, are added to the long and growing list of regulados — people who are prohibited from leaving the country. The latest to be added to this list is Pastor Velmis Adriana Medina Mariño, a member of the Apostolic Churches in Cuba.

In taking these measures against courageous critics, the regime seeks to reinforce its message that dissent will not be tolerated. These actions may backfire, however. A large majority of Cubans profess religious faith, and as many as 70% identify with a specific church. Moreover, Cuba's nuns, priests, pastors and other faith leaders of various traditions are trusted and respected voices in their communities. They are typically at the front lines, providing spiritual and material support to beleaguered people, and they are often among those calling for respect for human rights and dignity.

The movement we see today was started by the Cuban people, and the course of the nation is in their hands. But the U.S. and other pro-democracy international actors can and should do what they can to help. One way to help immediately is through providing desperately needed humanitarian assistance. After the protests began, the Cuban government announced that it will temporarily lift restrictions on some goods brought by travelers to the island. However, this is a limited and mostly symbolic measure since it only applies to a few suitcases of products per week given the paucity of daily flights from the U.S. to Havana. Government-imposed impediments on the bulk of potential humanitarian assistance that can be donated and distributed by U.S.

and other donors remain in place.

If and when the opportunity to meaningfully send assistance arrives, donors must be smart in how they go about delivering aid. In a letter sent recently to the Biden administration, U.S. Sen. Marco Rubio called for humanitarian assistance for the Cuban people through "trustworthy and independent international organizations." This is an important requirement because the Cuban government is a predatory regime that seeks to take advantage of any funds or assistance that enters the island to enrich itself.

The organization I lead, Outreach Aid to the Americas (OAA), is one of numerous nonprofits with experience facilitating the delivery of humanitarian assistance to Cubans in need. We partner with churches and ministries in the U.S. and in Cuba to ship containers carrying meal packs, hygiene and COVID- 19 related products, and other needed materials that reach the intended recipients in part because of the independence of the organizations that we work with.

At OAA, we also advocate for freedom of thought, conscience and religion or belief as a foundational human right essential for a free society. Additional vaccines and more food will offer real relief, but as long as people are unable to march freely, criticize their leaders or practice their faith without fear, they will continue taking to the streets chanting "Patria y Vida" (Homeland and Life), demanding the freedom they have been denied for too long.

Miami Herald

On Oct. 10, say a prayer for Cuba and the destiny of its people.
BY TEO BABÚN
OCTOBER 05, 2021

Someday Cuba will be free. And when it is, July 11, 2021, will be remembered as the day that Cubans across the country spoke with one voice about their desire for freedom, basic human needs and political reform. Spontaneous, peaceful demonstrations spread to more than

60 cities and towns across the island. The world heard their cries, but so did Cuba's government and Communist Party rulers. Within hours, protesters were confronted by police and paramilitary units. Some were beaten, and hundreds were detained. Many still languish in Cuba's deplorable prisons. The regime's message was clear – dissent will not be tolerated, no matter how desperate the living conditions, no matter its failure to provide essential health services and no matter how demoralized Cubans have become as their human rights have been stripped away.

In Cuba — and other countries that have faced the consequences of authoritarian dictatorships, the downtrodden find comfort — and solutions — through their faith. Despite the constant harassment of Cuba's churches, including by the Communist Party's enforcer, the Office of Religious Affairs (ORA), millions of Cubans worship and receive spiritual guidance from their religious leaders. Their churches fill the void in community social-service delivery as the government fails in that role and have become centers for dialogue and activism. But the government sows' discord between churches that fall under an official caste system, including registered churches whose operations are tolerated and unregistered churches that must operate in the shadows. ORA drives wedges between religious communities to ensure each is isolated and collectively cannot threaten the regime.

History teaches us that there are two paths to freedom when faced with tyrannical rule. We can take up arms and fight for our God-given rights, but that road is inevitably paved in blood. Or we can follow the examples of Mahatma Gandhi and Martin Luther King, who showed that unity, nonviolent dissent, and constructive dialogue can achieve the same ends. Gandhi succeeded in and India (human rights and political independence), and King brought about civil rights reforms in the United States.

In the aftermath of July 11, a dynamic nucleus of church leaders is uniting, for the first time, through an initiative called Cristianos Cubanos en Comunión. "C3" is a broad coalition of Catholic and Protestant leaders that share a common vision, including Christian evangelization and a collective "search for liberty, truth and goodness." As a first step, they are inviting all Cubans and friends of Cuba, on the island and abroad, to take action through an International Day of Prayer and fasting for Cuba on Sunday, Oct. 10.

Their call is inspired by their cross-denominational belief in the transformative power of God to bring peaceful, positive, life-giving change to Cuba. And in a country where civil society is repressed, it represents a major collective action outside the control of Cuba's repressive government. I recently met with members of C3 — all of whom have been targeted and persecuted by the Cuban government. I was impressed by their resolve: "Si se meten con uno, se meten con todos!" ("If they mess with one of us, they mess with all of us!") Such unity within the faith community is exactly what the Cuban government does not want. But the will of those who see through a lens of faith cannot be regulated or suppressed. Members of C3 unveiled a video of their unity in a prayer at bit.ly/39M4Gnq. It's an impressive beginning. Their initiative deserves international support. I urge all to pray on Oct. 10 — for Cuba, the unity of its people and its path to democracy, human rights, and prosperity.

Teo A. Babún is president & CEO of Outreach Aid to the Americas, Inc.

Read this Op-Ed online at:
www.miamiherald.com/opinion/op-edarticle254788852.html#storylink=cpy

OPINION

Does Pope Francis care about Nicaraguan Catholics?
by Teo Babún
September 01, 2022 12:00 AM

More than two dozen member states of the Organization of American States last month approved a resolution condemning the authoritarian government of Daniel Ortega in Nicaragua for its crackdown on civil society, the independent press, and, notably, Catholic clergy and institutions. This is a welcome development, given a shocking intensification in Ortega's persecution of the Catholic Church.

In April 2018, when the Ortega regime violently cracked down on mass protests throughout Nicaragua, Catholic leaders defied the regime by criticizing its human rights abuses and opening their churches to those fleeing deadly attacks by security and paramilitary forces. This, in turn, provoked a government campaign of systematic church repression and the demonization of its clergy (state media outlets regularly call priests "terrorists" and "devils in cassocks"). All hopes of democratic reform were dashed when Ortega locked up his political opponents in 2021 and stole the November elections.

This year has seen an all-out war against Catholic leaders. In March, the Ortega regime expelled Archbishop Waldemar Stanislaw Sommertag, the apostolic nuncio since 2018, giving him a week to leave. In May, police and paramilitary groups prevented Rev. Harving Padilla and parishioners in Masaya from leaving or entering a church for three days. Later in May, Rev. Manuel Garcia was detained after he

wielded a machete as he tried to fend off pro-regime thugs taunting and insulting him outside his parish. He was later sentenced by a court to two years in prison, making him the first priest imprisoned since the 2018 protests.

In its zealous persecution of the Catholic Church, the Ortega regime has also gone after the church's educational and charitable institutions. This year alone, the regime has forcibly closed more than 1,000 civil society organizations, many of which are Catholic. In June, the regime canceled the legal status of the Missionaries of Charity, an order founded by Mother Teresa of Calcutta, and expelled the nuns, escorting them to the Costa Rican border.

One priest who has particularly drawn the Ortega regime's ire is Monsignor Rolando Alvarez, bishop of the Diocese of Matagalpa, who is one of the most vocal critics of the regime's human rights abuses.

Earlier this summer, he went on a hunger strike to protest his treatment and the closure of seven Catholic radio stations that he directed. Then, a few weeks ago, he and 10 others, including seminarians and lay persons, were placed under house arrest in the episcopal offices. The police announced an investigation of Alvarez and other Catholic leaders for using communications platforms and social media to organize and incite acts of hatred and disturbing the peace.

The bishop has remained firm, insisting he has no intention of leaving the country and using his plight to urge the faithful to be courageous in the face of an antagonistic and brutal regime. He regularly transmitted video messages offering words of encouragement and assurance to his sympathizers. He said simply, "Our lives are in the hands of the Lord."

The OAS resolution demonstrates the seriousness in which regional stakeholders view the tragic and unacceptable situation in Nicaragua. The U.S. government joined in condemning the Ortega regime's actions: Ambassador-at-Large for Religious Freedom Rashad Hussein called on the regime to "end repression of Catholic clergy." Troublingly, one important voice has remained largely muted — that of Pope Francis. The silence from the Vatican for weeks since the crackdown on Nicaraguan Catholic leaders provoked cries of frustration: A group of Nicaraguans in exile penned a letter to Pope Francis urging him to speak out against the Ortega regime. This silence was especially painful given the Vatican's, and particularly the pope's, tremendous moral authority in Latin America.

Finally, on Aug. 21, Pope Francis expressed "concern" about the situation and said he desired to see a "sincere and open dialogue" between the government and the opposition. This statement demonstrates either an inexcusable ignorance about the true nature of the Ortega regime, which is incapable of engaging in the kind of dialogue that is needed to bring positive change, or a disappointing timidity. What the Nicaraguan faithful need now from the pope is a clear denunciation and expression of solidarity. They need to know that the leader of their church is firmly on their side.

Teo A. Babun is the president and CEO of Outreach Aid to the Americas, a faith- based nonprofit organization dedicated to serving vulnerable communities in the Americas through humanitarian and development assistance and human rights advocacy.

Miami Herald

Cuba and Nicaragua on US list of worst violators of religious freedom.
They deserve it. - Guest Opinion

By Teo A. Babun December 08, 2022

On Dec. 2, the U.S. Department of State designated Cuba and Nicaragua "Countries of Particular Concern (CPC)," a list of the worst violators of religious freedom.

CPC countries are those that "engage in or tolerate particularly severe violations of religious freedom," as established by the International Religious Freedom Act of 1998. Also on this list are China, North Korea and Saudi Arabia, whose repressive tactics the dictators of Cuba and Nicaragua seem eager to emulate.

Cuba and Nicaragua certainly deserve their place on this list. As their repression of civil society, dissidents and human rights activists has grown more brutal and brazen, their targeting of religious persons, including pastors, priests, and nuns, has likewise intensified.

In Nicaragua, the regime of Daniel Ortega has persecuted the Catholic Church since the mass protests of April 2018, when church leaders criticized the regime's violent crackdown and offered their churches as safe havens to protesters. Since the Catholic Church defied the regime in this way, its bishops, priests and lay people have been slandered and demonized, harassed, intimidated and jailed on trumped up charges. One courageous church leader, Bishop Rolando Álvarez, has been under house arrest for more than 100 days. Other priests, seminarians and lay leaders are in prison awaiting sentencing.

The Ortega regime has also gone after various institutions of the church, shutting down universities, schools and hospitals, and expelling from the country the Religious Sisters of the Cross and the Missionaries of Charity, the order founded by Mother Teresa. A recently published report by Nicaraguan lawyer Martha Patricia Molina shows that since 2018, the Catholic Church in Nicaragua has suffered 396 attacks, 127 this year alone. This led the Organization of American States to pass a resolution in August condemning the Ortega regime's harassment of the Catholic Church and its members.

In Cuba, the communist regime's systematic persecution of the island's independent faith community is well known. As the human rights situation there has deteriorated, especially following last year's historic July 11 mass protests, the regime has aggressively targeted religious leaders and their churches that denounce repression and call for justice for those who have been unjustly imprisoned.

Cuban state security continues to intimidate, harass, threaten and imprison openly critical religious leaders, even in the face of strong international condemnation. For instance, In and official expressions of concern by high-level UN human rights monitors.

When independent faith leaders refuse to be silenced, the Cuban regime has turned to expulsion. For instance, Pastor Alain Toledano, an Afro-Cuban leader in Cuba's Apostolic Movement, left the island in July with his family after being told he would be imprisoned if he did not leave within 30 days. Another recent expulsion was that of Father David Pantaleón, the superior of the Jesuits in Cuba. Authorities did not renew his residency permit (he is Dominican) after he refused to silence Jesuits on the island who were criticizing the regime.

The State Department's CPC designation of Cuba and Nicaragua is well earned, but also validates the importance of monitoring, documenting and reporting on violations of religious freedom. This work is being done by numerous organizations, including the one I lead, but it can only continue with the support of international partners and donors. Now is not the time to let up pressure, because we can be certain that the dictators in Cuba and Nicaragua do not intend to let up their pressure on people who simply seek to exercise their fundamental rights.

Teo A. Babun is the president and CEO of Outreach Aid to the Americas, a faith-based nonprofit organization dedicated to serving vulnerable communities in the Americas through humanitarian and development assistance and human rights advocacy.

Miami Herald

Nicaraguan bishop stayed behind, a symbol of brave defiance to the Ortega dictatorship | Opinion

By Teo A. Babun

March 02, 2023 9:09 Am

While her husband, President Daniel Ortega, was out of the country in April

2018, Nicaragua's Vice President Rosario Murillo announced a set of punitive social reforms that provoked a massive popular backlash.

Upon his return, Ortega launched a harsh crackdown that led to hundreds of deaths, the arrests of more than 1,000 dissidents, and the closing of independent media outlets and thousands of civil society organizations.

In the run-up to the November 2021 elections, Ortega arrested all opposition presidential candidates, who, along with other political prisoners, suffered inhumane conditions in prison. By locking up his opponents and manipulating the electoral process and vote count, Ortega and Murillo swindled their way to a new term in office.

The reality, however, is that their popular support has collapsed given the hardships Nicaraguans face, and they only retain control through self-serving corruption, domination of state institutions and ruthless authoritarianism.

On Feb. 9, following a U.S.-led international campaign of criticism and sanctions that increasingly isolated Nicaragua, the regime released and deported 222 ex- candidates and other political prisoners to the United States. The now-stateless ex-prisoners have been speaking out about the abuse they suffered and their dreams of a democratic Nicaragua.

After their release, Ortega's puppet National Assembly stripped the former prisoners of their Nicaraguan citizenship and moved to confiscate their property. Days later, the regime, without offering any evidence, stripped the nationality and confiscated the assets of another 94 individuals accused of working to undermine the nation's sovereignty.

These are serious human-rights violations — all governments must uphold the rule of law and respect citizens' rights, including due process, citizenship, and property rights.

The prisoner release does not resolve a larger pattern of human-rights abuses, including at least 35 political prisoners still behind bars, the most visible being Monsignor Rolando Álvarez, the bishop of Matagalpa.

Álvarez, a leading regime critic, had the chance to leave the country with the other political prisoners. But he told his captors he wanted to consult with the other bishops first. The regime refused and the next day sentenced him to 26 years for treason and other trumped-up charges. He was remanded to the maximum security infiernillo (little hell) lockup at La Modelo Prison. The name says it all — Ortega-Murillo want to break Álvarez for not submitting to them and will risk making him a martyr.

Ortega, rumored to have health issues, referred to his wife in a Feb. 13 speech as "co-president" and says he will change the constitution to reflect her promotion. But Murillo — whom Ortega pointedly credited with the prisoner- release scheme — is even less popular than her husband. While there are nine Catholic priests imprisoned for denouncing the regime's abuses, Álvarez stands out as a high-ranking figure, appointed by Pope Benedict and defiant of the dictatorship.

What the "co-presidents" need least is for an inspirational national resistance figure to emerge, yet that is exactly what Álvarez has become in these past weeks. His mistreatment guarantees that the much-loved bishop will become an international symbol of the desire of Nicaraguans, who are overwhelmingly religious, for the return of a government that upholds justice and respects human rights.

Some may think the release of political prisoners calls for a relaxation in sanctions and diplomatic pressure by the United States and other international actors. This would be a mistake. As these latest injustices against Álvarez and the lawless stripping of citizenship and properties from Nicaraguans show, it's imperative to maintain pressure on the criminals in Managua.

My organization will continue to support these efforts through disseminating information on human-rights violations, monitoring legal changes that affect rights and raising awareness of Nicaragua's international human-rights obligations. Our aim is to help bring about accountability in Nicaragua.

Teo A. Babun is the president and CEO of Outreach Aid to the Americas.

𝕸𝖎𝖆𝖒𝖎 𝕳𝖊𝖗𝖆𝖑𝖉

Here's the most important thing Catholic bishops in Cuba should not concede to the regime | Opinion
Teo A. Babun
May 4, 2023

On April 27, the Conference of Catholic Bishops of Cuba held a meeting with senior officials of the Cuban communist regime, including President Miguel Díaz-Canel. Bishops had requested this meeting for more than two years, and it reportedly covered issues of common interest, including the socioeconomic crisis that afflicts the island.

Especially noteworthy, however, was that they discussed a potential release of prisoners jailed during the historic protests of July 11, 2021, when thousands of Cubans took to the streets to protest food shortages and power cuts, and to demand libertad. Of the hundreds imprisoned and prosecuted, several dozen are minors — a particularly flagrant injustice that has been widely denounced by the international community.

The possibility of a prisoner release was raised earlier this year during Italian Cardinal Benaimino Stella's visit. He conveyed Pope Francis' wishes for a "positive response" regarding the prisoners. Sadly, it is likely that Cuba's leaders see as a possible model what Nicaragua did with 222 of its high-profile political prisoners in February — deporting them to the United States and stripping them of their citizenship and property.

But the fact that the regime is discussing this with the bishops raises another troubling element: Cuban officials probably expect some kind of concession from the Catholic leaders. Add to this that Caridad Diego, who heads the notorious Office of Religious Affairs (ORA), —

responsible for regulating all matters dealing with religion on the island — was at the meeting.

ORA is also the primary apparatus used to repress the fundamental right to freedom of religion or belief. It has been well documented that the office refuses to recognize unregistered or disfavored religious groups and denies requests for permits for construction and to hold large events, for example.

Those who care about human rights, and specifically religious freedom in Cuba, should hope that the Cuban Catholic bishops do not bow to one concession that the ORA has likely asked for: the silencing of brave priests and nuns who have publicly spoken out against the regime's grave human-rights abuses.

(For public dissemination)
USCIRF Hearing: "Deteriorating Religious Freedom Conditions in Cuba"

Dr. Teo Babun
President and CEO, Outreach Aid to the Americas
Wednesday, June 28, 2023

Mr. Chairman, Commissioners, thank you organizing this hearing on deteriorating religious freedom conditions in Cuba. Religious freedom is indeed under attack in Cuba, and I appreciate the commission shining a light on this reality, one that the Cuban regime frequently denies against all evidence to the contrary.

I especially want to commend you for recommending that the U.S. Department of State designate Cuba a "country of particularly concern," the category for the world's worst violators of religious freedom. Cuba doesn't get the headlines the way countries like China and Iran do, but it certainly has earned its place on this list. Thankfully the State Department has recognized this when it designated Cuba a CPC in November of last year.

It is an honor for me to appear before you as a witness and as President and CEO of Outreach Aid to the Americas, a faith-based organization dedicated to serving vulnerable people in the Americas. In Cuba, OAA focuses on humanitarian relief - including for individuals persecuted or imprisoned for their religious beliefs, support for defenders of religious freedom and other human rights, and other programs that advance the role of the faith community within Cuba's repressed civil society. Being headquartered in Miami, OAA works closely with the Cuban diaspora community - including recently exiled activists - to expand awareness of on-island needs and current trends and tactics of repression, and to encourage the continued engagement of the Cubans in exile in on-island human rights advocacy and democracy building programs.

OAA is pleased to have assisted USCIRF with logistics for this hearing, including in identifying the venue at the American Museum of the Cuban Diaspora, an outstanding facility dedicated to showcasing and documenting the history, culture, and contributions of the Cuban exile community.

In Cuba, as in other countries whose populations suffer rule by predatory authoritarians, the downtrodden often find comfort and practical help through their faith. Despite the constant harassment by the regime, millions of Cubans regularly worship and receive spiritual guidance from their religious leaders – though often they must do so from the shadows.

Even as they suffer the systematic violation of their religious freedom and constant attempts at division by a hostile regime, Cuba's faith communities have for many years been filling a crucial role within the island's civil society – providing hope and spiritual support as well as social services to a beleaguered people deprived of liberty and material resources. Faith leaders, moreover, have frequently stood and continue to stand at the front lines of human rights defense, promoting peaceful dialogue and advocating for non-violent change.

They do all this at great risk, however. As anyone who understands Cuba knows, the communist regime does not tolerate any criticism or challenge to its authority. As a Jewish leader said in a webinar that we hosted recently: "The communists tell you, 'You can believe in whatever you want, but you have to kneel in front of the dictatorship. You are going to believe, but I am going to put the limits on your belief.'"

To begin to understand the issue of religious freedom in Cuba, one must first know a little about the history of the Cuban communist regime's treatment of religion on the island. Following the 1959 revolution, Cuba declared itself an atheist state under the constitution and severely persecuted churches and other religious actors, expelling many of them from the island.

In time, the communist government took a more pragmatic position on the "religion problem," in part because it recognized that almost all Cubans professed religious faith. During Castro's rule, Cuba was visited by three Roman Catholic pontiffs – more than any other Latin American country – and in 1992, the regime relaxed restrictions on religious communities and, under a new constitution, declared Cuba a "secular state."

Despite the regime's relaxing some of its restrictions, it has continued to systematically violate Cubans' fundamental right to freedom of religion or belief. Indeed, the regime's policy toward religion is one of repression and tight control. This is especially the case with regard to unregistered (the regime considers them "illegal") religious groups, many of which are openly critical of the regime.

The Cuban constitution contains FoRB protections. Article 15 reads, "The State recognizes, respects, and guarantees religious freedom," and according to article 57, "Every person has the right to profess or not profess religious beliefs, to change these and to practice his or her religion of preference, with due respect to the others and in conformity with the law." This is in Cuba's new constitution, approved by referendum in 2019. It is in fact weaker on religious freedom because it omits language protecting this right that had been in the last constitution, from 1992, such as the term "freedom of conscience."

Cuba does not have a constitutionally based rule of law. In practice, the constitution is subordinate to a battery of administrative and legal codes and decrees used to violate FoRB and other fundamental rights under the cover of punishing crime and of upholding "revolutionary ideals." In fact, the regime sees not only religious activists, but any religious leader who publicly criticizes it, as "counter-revolutionaries" who must be controlled and made an example of.

The primary vehicle of repression is the government's Office of Religious Affairs (ORA), which is responsible for regulating religious activity on the island. ORA is part of the Central Committee of the ruling Communist Party, and it has authority on all matters related to religious groups, including their registration, travel outside the country, and building and construction permits. ORA applies rules in an arbitrary manner, showing favoritism to religious groups that are seen as cooperative or supportive of the government, while harassing those that are critical of the regime and that insist on maintaining their organizational independence.

Other tactics used to repress religious groups are: harassment, threats and physical attacks on faith leaders and parishioners; confiscation of property; frequent police summons; defamation and accusations of illegal or immoral behavior; denial of rights of employment or education, including for family members; acts of repudiation; the use of "public opinion agents" to sow rumors; creation of enmity and division between faith groups; restrictions on free movement; and fabrication of alleged crimes followed by fines and detention. The authorities also used the COVID-19 pandemic as a pretext to infringe on FoRB rights.

The Miami Herald

Religious Freedom Week helped highlight Cubans Pay dearly for living their faith.
By Teo A. Babun
July 5, 2023

The United States conference of Catholic Bishops recently observed Religious Freedom Week, a time to "pray, reflect and act to promote religious freedom," as its website reads.

The observance considers religious freedom in the United State and abroad. In view of this, it is fitting that the U.S Commission on International Religious

Freedom (USCIRF) held a hearing that same week on worsening religious freedom conditions in Cuba. Held at the American Museum of the Cuban Diaspora in Little Havana in Miami, this was the commission's first hearing outside of Washington, D.C.

As the president of Outreach Aid to the Americas (OAA), a faith-based non-profit organization in Miami that works to empower and advocate for fundamental freedoms in Cuba, Nicaragua, and Venezuela, among others, I was privileged to testify at this hearing.

I shared that, in Cuba, leaders of various faith traditions are frequently on the front lines of human-rights defense, promoting peaceful dialogue and advocating for democratic change. They do this at great risk because they face constant surveillance, harassment and threats by state security agents charged with carrying out a policy of control and repression of religion on the island.

A poll released recently by the Madrid-based human rights monitor **Observatorio Cubano de Derechos Humanos** showed that 68% of Cubans on the island know someone who has been harassed, repressed, threatened, or obstructed in their daily life for reasons related to their faith.

The survey concludes that religious freedoms are not respected or guaranteed in Cuba. The regime continues to use its surveillance and control systems to limit public expression by those who assume a political or civic posture inspired by faith. As a Cuban Jewish leader said in a webinar we hosted recently: "The [Cuban] communists tell you, 'You can believe in whatever you want, but you have to kneel in front of the dictatorship. You are going to believe, but I am going to put limits on your belief.' "By its nature, religious belief deals with ultimate things and ultimate authority, one who has a lot to say about truth, justice, and the responsibilities of earthly rulers. But Cuba's communist regime brooks no competitors to its authority, and it will not tolerate criticism.

In my testimony, I recommended to the U.S Department of State and the international community the following: Keep Cuba on the State Department's list of "Countries of Particular Concern," its list of the world's worst violators of religious freedom, unless conditions improve measurably (Cuba was placed on this list in 2022 for the first time a well-earned recognition of its brutality); impose new sanctions on officials orchestrating religious repression, including through denial of travel visas, as well as restrictions on international banking and investment; and continue to robustly fund programs to support Cubans in their struggle to ensure greater respect not only for religious freedom but also for such complementary fundamental rights as freedom of expression and freedom of assembly.

Also testifying on Wednesday was my friend, the brave Catholic priest Father

Rolando Montes de Oca, who lives in Cuba. In 2021, when a journalist asked him if he was afraid to speak freely despite living under totalitarianism, he replied: "I am afraid of not being true to my conscience. I am afraid of distancing myself from my people. I am afraid of listening to fears, and not to values, and not to God, and not to the cry of my people."

Cuba's communist rulers may have the power to hurt, jail and kill those who speak out against it, but men and women like Father Rolando show us that they have more power still: the power of faith that gives people strength and fuels their hope for a free and democratic future for their nation.

Teo A. Babun is the president and CEO of Outreach Aid to the Americas.

SECTION VIII

Freedom of Religion or Belief Defenders

"For genuine Christians, it is not enough to hold their faith in the privacy of their hearts and homes; it must guide and impact how and what they do in all of life."

Harry R. Jackson, Jr., Author
Personal Faith Public Policy

"Give justice to the weak and the fatherless; maintain the right of the afflicted and the destitute. Rescue the weak and the needy; deliver them from the hand of the wicked." Psalm 82:3-4 ESV

This section of the book tells the story of the Defenders of Freedom. These are the stories and testimonies of those who struggle for freedom in Cuba, Nicaragua, Venezuela, and elsewhere. These are some of the ones who suffer daily abuse by corrupt tyrants and dictators. These are the brave liberty seeking men and women who suffer under totalitarian and abusive governments; who suffer persecution against themselves, their families and their ministries; who are apprehended and jailed for breaking Machiavellian laws like "illegal association," and holding "illicit meetings." who are expelled from their own countries; who are branded as "terrorists;" who are deprived of their most basic liberties; and who, often with their families, face the full oppressive weight of governments determined to crush anyone who dares speak out and call evil by its name.

We understand better when we read the testimonies of these brave men and women.

The first story: On June 13th, 2023, I received an unexpected call via WhatsApp from an unknown number. The caller identified himself as Pastor Lorenzo Rosales Fajardo, from Cuba. At first, I was skeptical of the call, as I was aware of Pastor Rosales' situation. At the time, he was serving a 7-year imprisonment sentence and had become a symbol of the international campaign to free Cuban human rights activists.

In my line of work, I was familiar with his case, as we had been advocating for pastors who had been imprisoned due to their religious leadership roles. Pastor Rosales Fajardo was a trained Baptist minister and had served as the pastor and leader of the Monte de Sion independent church in Palma Soriano. On July 11, 2021, he and his son were detained and separated during a peaceful protest, and he was charged by the Cuban government.

The circumstances of his arrest were harrowing. Reports suggest that he was severely beaten and assaulted during his transfer to a state security facility in Santiago de Cuba, resulting in him losing a tooth. Furthermore, he was charged with public disorder, incitement, and assault. Throughout his detention, he was held incommunicado, and his family was repeatedly denied contact with him.

During our conversation, Pastor Rosales Fajardo expressed that he had been praying for me for the past 15 years. He also revealed that reaching out to me was something he was prohibited from doing due to being considered an enemy of the Cuban state. Our conversation left a profound impact on me, and I was humbled by his kind words and heartening personality. He shared with me that he had no hard feelings with his jailers; he felt no hate whatsoever and hoped that jailers and other prisoners would learn about the power of his (La mano de Dios); and the person of Jesus through him.

When I asked him what he needed most, his answer left me in tears. He simply requested something to get rid of the bed bugs or chinch bugs (chinchilla) in his prison cell so that he could sleep for more than a few hours each day. Heroes like Pastor Rosales Fajardo, who suffer for advocating freedom of religion, are truly special and inspiring individuals.

The second story: The following prayer was smuggled from a Chinese prison where Pastor Wang Yi was given a prison sentence of nine years by Chengdu Intermediate People's Court for "inciting subversion of state power and illegal business operations." The sentence also included the stripping of political rights for three years and confiscation of his personal assets.

"My Declaration of Faithful Disobedience"

"I hope God uses me, by means of first losing my personal freedom, to tell those who have deprived me of my personal freedom that there is an authority higher than their authority, and that there is a freedom that they cannot restrain, a freedom that fills the church of the crucified and risen Jesus Christ."

"Regardless of what crime the government charges me with, whatever filth they fling at me, as long as this charge is related to my faith, my writings, my comments, and my teachings, it is merely a lie and temptation of demons. I categorically deny it. I will serve my sentence, but I will not serve the law. I will be executed, but I will not plead guilty."

'Those who lock me up will one day be locked up by angels. Those who interrogate me will finally be questioned and judged by Christ. When I think of this, the Lord fills me with a natural compassion and grief toward those who are attempting to and actively imprisoning me. Pray that the Lord would use me, that he would grant me patience and wisdom, that I might take the gospel to them."

"Separate me from my wife and children, ruin my reputation.. destroy my life and my family-the authorities are capable of doing all of these things. However, no one in this world can force me to renounce my faith; no one can make me change my life; and no one can raise me from the dead." "Jesus is the Christ, son of the eternal, living God. He died for sinners and rose to life for us. He is my king and the king of the whole earth yesterday, today, and forever, i am his servant, and I am imprisoned because of this. I will resist in meekness those who resist God, and I will joyfully violate all laws that violate God's laws."

This section of the book of individual freedom of religion victims is dedicated to other brave and courageous defenders of freedom like Pastors Wang Yi and Lorenzo Rosales Fajardo.

Darvin Leiva

Nicaragua

- **Gender:** Male
- **Perpetrator:** Nicaragua
- **Religion or Belief:** Christian – Catholic
- **Sentence:** 10 Years' Imprisonment
- **Current Status:** Exiled
- **Religious Leader:** No
- **Most Recent Type of Abuse:** Imprisonment
- **Reason for Persecution:** Criticizing Religious Freedom Conditions Human Rights Work for Religious Communities Religious Activity
- **Nature of Charges:** Spreading Propaganda & False or Misleading Ideas, Information, or Materials Subversion

Darvin Leiva was imprisoned in relation to criticism of religious freedom conditions.

On August 4, 2022, police prevented several people, including Leiva, a seminarian, from leaving the residence of Bishop Rolando Álvarez as the bishop was on his way to perform mass at a local cathedral. Álvarez had criticized the government's recent closure of several Catholic radio stations and its human rights record. Alvarez, Leiva, and the other individuals in the residence remained under de facto house arrest as authorities investigated them for "organizing violent groups" and encouraging them "to carry out acts of hate against the population."

On August 19, 2022, police detained Leiva and sent him to the Evaristo Vásquez Sánchez Police Complex. On October 4, 2022, it was revealed that Leiva was charged with "conspiracy to undermine national integrity" and "propagation of false news."

On January 26, 2023, Leiva was reportedly found guilty. Prosecutors reportedly requested 10 years in prison.

On February 3, 2023, a judge from the Second Criminal District Court of Trials of Managua sentenced Leiva to 10 years in prison.

On February 9, 2023, Leiva was released from prison and exiled to the United States.

Donaida Pérez Paseiro

Cuba

Donaida Pérez Paseiro is imprisoned for her religious identity, religious activity, and religious leadership role. On July 16, 2021, Paseiro, the president of the Free Yoruba Association of Cuba (Asociación de Yorubas Libres de Cuba, or "Free Yorubas"), an independent Santería community, formally surrendered herself to police in compliance with an arrest warrant following her peaceful participation in protests on July 11, 2021. Paseiro was charged with public disorder, disobedience/contempt, and assault.

In September 2021, it was reported that Paseiro had been sentenced to eight years in prison; however, additional reporting from January 2022 indicated that she was still on trial and had yet to be officially sentenced. Prosecutors were reportedly seeking eight years in prison for Paseiro.

In December 2021, Paseiro was transferred to a hospital after vomiting blood and experiencing abdominal pain for two days. '
On an unspecified date, Paseiro was reportedly sentenced to eight years in prison.

In late July 2022, Paseiro reportedly developed COVID-19 symptoms and was forced to isolate.
Prison authorities have reportedly tried to force Paseiro to renounce her faith.

Paseiro is currently being held in Guamajal Prison, Villa Clara. Paseiro is married with two children. Her husband Loreto Hernández García is also imprisoned for his participation in July 11 protests.

Paseiro has been repeatedly harassed by authorities because of her religious leadership role. In September 2020, she was arrested and assaulted by police, sustaining injuries to her chest and face. She was also arrested in February 2020.

- **Gender:** Female
- **Current Location:** Guamajal Prison, Villa Clara
- **Perpetrator:** Cuba
- **Ethnic Group:** Yoruba
- **Religion or Belief:** Santería
- **Health Concerns:** Hypertension, diabetes, contracted COVID-19
- **Sentence:** 8 Years' Imprisonment
- **Date of Detainment:** July/16/2021
- **Current Status:** In prison
- **Religious Leader:** Yes
- **Most Recent Type of Abuse:** Imprisonment
- **Reason for Persecution:** Religious Association Religious Figure & Religious Leadership Role Religious Identity
- **Nature of Charges:** Assault & Battery Public Disorder Unlawful Disobedience

Enrique Martínez

Nicaragua

- **Gender:** Male
- **Perpetrator:** Nicaragua
- **Religion or Belief:** Christian – Catholic
- **Health Concerns:** Diabetes, hypertension, kidney problems, blood circulation problems
- **Current Status:** Exiled
- **Religious Leader:** Yes
- **Most Recent Type of Abuse:** Detainment
- **Reason for Persecution:** Criticizing Religious Freedom Conditions Human Rights Work for Religious Communities Religious Figure & Religious Leadership Role
- **Nature of Charges:** Criminal Premeditation & Conspiracy Spreading Propaganda & False or Misleading Ideas, Information, or Materials

Enrique Martínez was detained for his religious leadership role.

On October 13, 2022, authorities reportedly violently arrested Martínez, the parish priest of St. Martha's Church in Managua, at his home. Riot police reportedly entered his home forcibly, broke down the door to his room, beat him, and pushed him into a van. Martínez was reportedly charged with conspiracy and propagating false news. Martínez's arrest came amid a crackdown of fellow clergymen criticizing the government for its human rights violations, including religious freedom.
On February 9, 2023, Martínez was released from prison and exiled to the United States.

Martínez reportedly suffers from diabetes, hypertension, kidney problems, and blood circulation problems.

Lisdiani and Lisdani Rodriguez Isaac

Cuba

- **Gender:** Female
- **Current Location:** Guamajal Prison, Villa Clara
- **Perpetrator:** Cuba
- **Ethnic Group:** Yoruba
- **Religion or Belief:** Santería
- **Sentence:** 8 Years' Imprisonment
- **Current Status:** In prison
- **Religious Leader:** No
- **Most Recent Type of Abuse:** Imprisonment
- **Reason for Persecution:** Religious Association Religious Identity
- **Nature of Charges:** Assault & Battery Public Disorder Unlawful Disobedience

Lisdiani Rodríguez Isaac and Lisdani Rodríguez Isaac are imprisoned in relation to them religious identity and activity.

On July 15, 2021, authorities detained Rodriguez Isaac, a member of the Free Yoruba Association of Cuba (Asociación de Yorubas Libres de Cuba, or "Free Yorubas"), an independent Santería community, alongside her twin sister, Lisdani Rodríguez Isaac, following their peaceful participation in protests on July 11, 2021. Rodriguez Isaac sisters were charged with public disorder, disobedience, and assault.

In September 2021, it was reported that Rodriguez Isaac sisters had been sentenced to ten years in prison; however, additional reporting from January 2022 indicated that them were currently on trial and had not been officially sentenced. Prosecutors were reportedly seeking ten years in prison for Lisdiani and Lisdani.

In March 2022, it was reported that Rodriguez Isaac sisters had been sentenced to eight years in prison. Lisdiani and Lisdani are currently being held in Guamajal Prison.

Lorenzo Rosales Fajardo

Cuba

Lorenzo Rosales Fajardo is imprisoned in relation to his religious leadership role.

On July 11, 2021, Rosales Fajardo, pastor and leader of the Monte de Sion Independent Church in Palma Soriano, and members of his church participated in peaceful protests in Palma Soriano. When police and the military tried to block protestors from marching, Rosales Fajardo and his son, David Lorenzo Rosales Carballo, were detained and separated. His son was released on July 17, 2021. Rosales Fajardo was initially held for a month in a state security facility in Santiago. During his transfer there, he was reportedly severely beaten which caused him to lose a tooth. During that same attack, it is reported that the guards also urinated on him. Rosales Fajardo was reportedly charged with disrespect, public disorder, incitement, and assault. Rosales Fajardo was also held incommunicado for most of his detention, and his family has been repeatedly denied contact with him.

On August 7, 2021, Rosales Fajardo's wife, Maridilegnis Carballo, was finally allowed to speak with him for a three minute phone call. She had previously been blocked from bringing him food and hygiene items there.

On August 9, 2021, Rosales Fajardo was reportedly transferred to the Boniato Maximum Security Prison, outside Santiago de Cuba.

On October 22, 2021, it was learned that prosecutors are seeking to imprison Rosales Fajardo for ten years.

On an unspecified date following his trial on December 20 and 21, 2021, Rosales Fajardo was sentenced to eight years in prison.
In May 2022, it was reported that Rosales Fajardo's sentence was reduced by a year to seven years in prison.
In June 2022, it was reported that Rosales Fajardo's appeal had been rejected.

On December 24, 2022, Rosales Fajardo was reportedly transferred from Boniato Maximum Security Prison to La Caoba, a minimum security prison in Palma Soriano.
Rosales Fajardo's wife has been threatened with imprisonment herself if she continues to speak out publicly about her husband's case.

Authorities have previously harassed Rosales Fajardo in relation to his religious activity. In 2012, they confiscated his church's property.

- **Gender:** Male
- **Current Location:** La Caoba
- **Perpetrator:** Cuba
- **Religion or Belief:** Christian – Protestant
- **Spouse or Dependents:** Yes
- **Sentence:** 7 Years' Imprisonment
- **Current Status:** In prison
- **Religious Leader:** Yes
- **Most Recent Type of Abuse:** Imprisonment
- **Reason for Persecution:** Religious Figure & Religious Leadership Role
- **Nature of Charges:** Assault & Battery Incitement to Commit Crime & Violence Public Disorder Unlawful Disobedience

Loreto Hernández García

Cuba

Loreto Hernández García is imprisoned for his religious identity, religious activity, and religious leadership role.
On July 15, 2021, authorities arrested García, vice president of the Free Yoruba Association of Cuba (Asociación de Yorubas Libres de Cuba, or "Free Yorubas"), an independent Santería community, following his peaceful participation in protests on July 11, 2021.

In May 2022, it was reported that García's health has severely deteriorated in prison as authorities fail to provide him food that takes into consideration his diabetes. It was also reported that García had been sentenced to seven years in prison on an unspecified date for public disorder, contempt, assault, and resistance.

On October 26, 2022, García requested permission to receive medical treatment outside of prison for symptoms believed to be consistent with pancreatic cancer.
On March 19, 2023, the Ministry of the Interior reportedly informed García that his request to receive medical treatment outside of prison had been refused.

In May 2023, it was reported that prison authorities committed acts of violence against García and placed him in a punishment cell for nearly eight hours. It was further reported that prison authorities continue to deny García the medical treatment he requires for his diabetes, hypertension, and heart disease diagnoses.
Prison authorities have reportedly tried to force García to renounce his faith.
García is married with two children. His wife Donaida Pérez Paseiro is also in prison for her participation in July 11 protests.

García reportedly suffers from several health conditions, including high blood pressure, asthma, hypertension, diabetes, and other cardiac issues that put his health at risk as he stays in prison. There are reports that García has been repeatedly denied proper medical care and that prison guards have used violence against him.
García was reportedly transferred from La Pendiente Prison, Santa Clara, to Provincial Prison.
García has reportedly been harassed repeatedly by authorities in the past because of his religious leadership role.

- **Gender:** Male
- **Current Location:** Provincial Prison, Santa Clara
- **Perpetrator:** Cuba
- **Ethnic Group:** Yoruba
- **Religion or Belief:** Santería
- **Health Concerns:** Asthma, Diabetes, Hypertension, High Blood Pressure, Other Cardiac Issues
- **Sentence:** 7 Years' Imprisonment
- **Current Status:** In prison
- **Religious Leader:** Yes
- **Most Recent Type of Abuse:** Imprisonment
- **Reason for Persecution:** Religious Association Religious Figure & Religious Leadership Role Religious Identity
- **Nature of Charges:** Assault & Battery Public Disorder Unlawful Disobedience

Melkin Sequeira

Nicaragua

Melkin Sequeira was imprisoned in relation to criticism of religious freedom conditions.

On August 4, 2022, police prevented several people, including Sequeira, a seminarian, from leaving the residence of Bishop Rolando Álvarez as the bishop was on his way to perform mass at a local cathedral. Álvarez had criticized the government's recent closure of several Catholic radio stations and its human rights record. Alvarez, Sequeira, and the other individuals in the residence remained under de facto house arrest as authorities investigated them for "organizing violent groups" and encouraging them "to carry out acts of hate against the population."

On August 19, 2022, police detained Sequeira and sent him to the Evaristo Vásquez Sánchez Police Complex. On October 4, 2022, it was revealed that Sequeira was charged with "conspiracy to undermine national integrity" and "propagation of false news."

On January 26, 2023, Sequeira was reportedly found guilty. Prosecutors reportedly requested 10 years in prison.

On February 3, 2023, a judge from the Second Criminal District Court of Trials of Managua sentenced Sequeira to 10 years in prison.

On February 9, 2023, Sequeira was released from prison and exiled to the United States.

- **Gender:** Male
- **Perpetrator:** Nicaragua
- **Religion or Belief:** Christian – Catholic
- **Sentence:** 10 Years' Imprisonment
- **Current Status:** Exiled
- **Religious Leader:** No
- **Most Recent Type of Abuse:** Imprisonment
- **Reason for Persecution:** Criticizing Religious Freedom Conditions Human Rights Work for Religious Communities Religious Activity
- **Nature of Charges:** Spreading Propaganda & False or Misleading Ideas, Information, or Materials Subversion

Oscar Benavidez

Nicaragua

- **Gender**: Male
- **Perpetrator**: Nicaragua
- **Religion or Belief:** Christian – Catholic
- **Sentence:** 10 Years' Imprisonment
- **Current Status:** Exiled
- **Religious Leader:** Yes
- **Most Recent Type of Abuse:** Imprisonment
- **Reason for Persecution:** Criticizing Religious Freedom Conditions Giving, Sharing, & Listening to a Religious Speech Human Rights Work for Religious Communities Religious Figure & Religious Leadership Role
- **Nature of Charges:** Spreading Propaganda & False or Misleading Ideas, Information, or Materials Subversion

Oscar Benavidez was imprisoned for criticizing religious freedom conditions.

On August 14, 2022, authorities reportedly arrested Benavidez, a priest, after he performed mass. Benavidez regularly condemned "injustices" committed by the government. During the mass prior to his arrest, he mentioned the persecution of the prophets. His arrest came amid a crackdown on Catholic religious figures and institutions throughout the country.

On January 16, 2023, the Tenth Court of the Criminal Trial District of Managua found Benavidez guilty of "conspiracy to undermine national security and sovereignty" and "spreading fake news." Prosecutors requested that Benavidez be sentenced to eight years in prison.

On January 24, 2023, Benavidez was sentenced to 10 years in prison.

On February 9, 2023, Benavidez was released from prison and exiled to the United States.

Ramiro Tijerino

Nicaragua

Ramiro Tijerino was imprisoned in relation to criticism of religious freedom conditions.

On August 4, 2022, police prevented several people, including Tijerino, a priest, from leaving the residence of Bishop Rolando Álvarez as the bishop was on his way to perform mass at a local cathedral. Álvarez had criticized the government's recent closure of several Catholic radio stations and its human rights record. Alvarez, Tijerino, and the other individuals in the residence remained under de facto house arrest as authorities investigated them for "organizing violent groups" and encouraging them "to carry out acts of hate against the population."

On August 19, 2022, police detained Tijerino and sent him to the Evaristo Vásquez Sánchez Police Complex. On October 4, 2022, it was revealed that Tijerino was charged with "conspiracy to undermine national integrity" and "propagation of false news."
On January 26, 2023, Tijerino was reportedly found guilty. Prosecutors reportedly requested 10 years in prison.

On February 3, 2023, a judge from the Second Criminal District Court of Trials of Managua sentenced Tijerino to 10 years in prison.

On February 9, 2023, Tijerino was released from prison and exiled to the United States.

- **Gender:** Male
- **Perpetrator:** Nicaragua
- **Religion or Belief:** Christian – Catholic
- **Sentence:** 10 Years' Imprisonment
- **Current Status:** Exiled
- **Religious Leader:** Yes
- **Most Recent Type of Abuse:** Imprisonment
- **Reason for Persecution:** Criticizing Religious Freedom Conditions Human Rights Work for Religious Communities Religious Activity Religious Figure & Religious Leadership Role
- **Nature of Charges:** Spreading Propaganda & False or Misleading Ideas, Information, or Materials Subversion

Raúl Antonio Vega

Nicaragua

Antonio Vega was imprisoned in relation to criticism of religious freedom conditions.

On August 4, 2022, police prevented several people, including Antonio Vega, a deacon, from leaving the residence of Bishop Rolando Álvarez as the bishop was on his way to perform mass at a local cathedral. Álvarez had criticized the government's recent closure of several Catholic radio stations and its human rights record. Alvarez, González, and the other individuals in the residence Raúl remained under de facto house arrest as authorities investigated them for "organizing violent groups" and encouraging them "to carry out acts of hate against the population."

On August 19, 2022, police detained Antonio Vega and sent him to the Evaristo Vásquez Sánchez Police Complex.

On October 4, 2022, it was revealed that Antonio Vega was charged with "conspiracy to undermine national integrity" and "propagation of false news."

On January 26, 2023, Antonio Vega was reportedly found guilty. Prosecutors reportedly requested 10 years in prison.

On February 3, 2023, a judge from the Second Criminal District Court of Trials of Managua sentenced Antonio Vega to 10 years in prison.

On February 9, 2023, Antonio Vega was released from prison and exiled to the United States.

- **Gender:** Male
- **Perpetrator:** Nicaragua
- **Religion or Belief:** Christian – Catholic
- **Sentence:** 10 Years' Imprisonment
- **Current Status:** Exiled
- **Religious Leader:** Yes
- **Most Recent Type of Abuse:** Imprisonment
- **Reason for Persecution:** Criticizing Religious Freedom Conditions Human Rights Work for Religious Communities Religious Activity Religious Figure & Religious Leadership Role
- **Nature of Charges:** Spreading Propaganda & False or Misleading Ideas, Information, or Materials Subversion

Rolando Jose Alvarez

Nicaragua

Rolando Álvarez is imprisoned for criticizing religious freedom conditions.

On August 4, 2022, police prevented Álvarez, bishop of the Matagalpa diocese, from leaving his home to perform mass at a local cathedral after he criticized the government's recent closure of several Catholic radio stations and its human rights record. Álvarez remained under de facto house arrest as authorities investigated him for "organizing violent groups" and encouraging them "to carry out acts of hate against the population."

On August 19, 2022, police arrested Álvarez from his residence. It is reported that he was taken to Managua and placed under house arrest in his parents' home.'

In December 2022, a court ordered that Álvarez remain under house arrest on charges of "conspiracy" and "spreading false news." He was also accused of "damaging the Nicaraguan government and society."

On February 10, 2023, a court sentenced Álvarez to 26 years in prison after he declined to be exiled to the United States in a prisoner release the day before.

Álvarez was reportedly convicted of several charges, including treason, undermining national integrity and spreading false news. He was also fined and stripped of his citizenship.

Álvarez is imprisoned at Sistema Penitenciario Nacional Jorge Navarro in Tipitapa.

- **Gender:** Male
- **Current Location:** Sistema Penitenciario Nacional Jorge Navarro, Tipitapa
- **Perpetrator:** Nicaragua
- **Religion or Belief:** Christian – Catholic
- **Sentence:** 26 Years' Imprisonment
- **Current Status:** In prison
- **Religious Leader:** Yes
- **Most Recent Type of Abuse:** Imprisonment
- **Reason for Persecution:** Criticizing Religious Freedom Conditions Human Rights Work for Religious Communities Religious Activity Religious Figure & Religious Leadership Role
- **Nature of Charges:** Criminal Premeditation & Conspiracy Spreading Propaganda & False or Misleading Ideas, Information, or Materials Treason & Sedition

Sergio Cárdenas

Nicaragua

- **Gender:** Male
- **Perpetrator:** Nicaragua
- **Religion or Belief:** Christian – Catholic
- **Sentence:** 10 Years' Imprisonment
- **Current Status:** Exiled
- **Religious Leader:** No
- **Most Recent Type of Abuse:** Imprisonment
- **Reason for Persecution:** Criticizing Religious Freedom Conditions Human Rights Work for Religious Communities Religious Activity
- **Nature of Charges:** Spreading Propaganda & False or Misleading Ideas, Information, or Materials Subversion

Sergio Cárdenas was imprisoned in relation to criticism of religious freedom conditions.

On August 4, 2022, police prevented several people, including Cárdenas, a cameraman, from leaving the residence of Bishop Rolando Álvarez as the bishop was on his way to perform mass at a local cathedral. Álvarez had criticized the government's recent closure of several Catholic radio stations and its human rights record. Alvarez, Cárdenas, and the other individuals in the residence remained under de facto house arrest as authorities investigated them for "organizing violent groups" and encouraging them "to carry out acts of hate against the population."

On August 19, 2022, police detained Cárdenas and sent him to the Evaristo Vásquez Sánchez Police Complex. On October 4, 2022, it was revealed that Cárdenas was charged with "conspiracy to undermine national integrity" and "propagation of false news."

On January 26, 2023, Cárdenas was reportedly found guilty. Prosecutors reportedly requested 10 years in prison.

On February 3, 2023, a judge from the Second Criminal District Court of Trials of Managua sentenced Cárdenas to 10 years in prison.

On February 9, 2023, Cárdenas was released from prison and exiled to the United States.

Silvio Báez

Nicaragua

As auxiliary bishop of Managua he constantly denounced the human rights abuses in the country, such as the Mother's Day massacre, in which over 15 people were shot dead and 200 wounded in different protests across Nicaragua on Mother's Day in 2018.

Bishop Báez has been exiled for four years from Nicaragua at the request of Pope Francis, who in 2019 asked the bishop to leave the country to protect him from death threats from the regime of President Daniel Ortega. Nicaraguan citizens began protesting Ortega in 2014 over political corruption, with tensions escalating over the next decade.

In the time leading up to his exile, Bishop Báez and other Catholic leaders served as intermediaries between Ortega and anti-government protesters. But in April 2018 the Ortega crackdown on protests turned deadly. As violence and killings escalated, the bishop became increasingly vocal in his criticism of the repressive government, and Ortega accused him of plotting a coup in October of 2018.

After leaving Nicaragua, Bishop Báez remained in Rome temporarily before moving to Miami, where he now resides and teaches at St. Vincent de Paul Seminary in Boynton Beach and celebrates that weekly Mass at St. Agatha which is livestreamed via Facebook to Nicaragua.

Throughout his painful exile, the bishop has maintained a razor-sharp focus on the unfolding crisis in his own country, analyzing the shifting tactics that the government has employed to tap the power of faith in a deeply pious nation.

- **Gender:** Male
- **Perpetrator:** Nicaragua
- **Religion or Belief:** Christian – Catholic
- **Current Status:** Exiled
- **Religious Leader:** Yes
- **Most Recent Type of Abuse:** Beaten by a pro-government mob while making a pastoral visit to the Minor Basilica of St. Sebastian in Diriamba in July 2018. Forced to exile due death threats in April 2019. Nicaraguan nationality revoked in February 2023.
- **Nature of charges:** Considered traitor to the homeland by the Nicaraguan Government. Subject to penalties that encompass both absolute and special disqualifications, which include the forfeiting of his citizenship rights in perpetuity.

Edwin Román

Nicaragua

- **Gender:** Male
- **Current location:** Miami, Florida
- **Perpetrator:** Nicaragua
- **Religion or Belief:** Christian Catholic
- **Status:** Exiled
- **Religious Leader:** Yes
- **Reason for persecution:** Accused of murder by setting fire to citizens who were killed during the April 2018 protests, and of encouraging the torture of policemen and having them set ablaze while they were alive.
- **Nature of charges:** Considered traitor to the homeland by the Nicaraguan Government. Subject to penalties that encompass both absolute and special disqualifications, which include the forfeiting of his citizenship rights in perpetuity.

Catholic priest Edwin Román -one of the most critical priests in Nicaragua- arrived in Miami on August 3, 2021, for a brief stay with only a small carry-on suitcase. But the following day, Nicaraguan Vice President Rosario Murillo, wife of President Daniel Ortega, called him a murderer and his plans changed. He listened to his parish's faithful and decided to stay in exile.

Father Román not only witnessed the repression of the police forces in April 2018, when the popular uprising took place, he suffered it firsthand. He saw the mothers who lost their children cry, he provided assistance to the young people who were repressed in Masaya, he managed and obtained the release of several detainees who participated in the demonstrations.

In February 2019, he was arrested, beaten and later released by the Masaya Police. In November of the same year, a police contingent besieged his parish, and he remained locked up providing accompaniment to relatives of political prisoners who began a hunger strike to demand the release of prisoners of conscience. For nine days, those inside the parish had no running water and no electricity; both were cut off in an attempt to subdue them. The confinement left after-effects on his health, to the point that he had to use a cane to regain stability.

Father Román was forced to exile due death threats in August 2021. His Nicaraguan nationality was revoked in February 2023.

Manuel Garcia

Nicaragua

- **Gender:** Male
- **Current location:** Direccion de Auxilio Judicial (known as Chipote)
- **Perpetrator:** Nicaragua
- **Religion or Belief:** Christhian Catholic
- **Sentence:** 2 years imprisonment and 200 days fine equivalent to $386 US dollars (14,116 Córdobas local currency).
- **Date of Detainment:** 6/1/2022
- **Current Status:** In prison
- **Religious Leader:** Yes
- **Reason for persecution:** Nicaraguan Government maneuvers of sexual scandal, trials, and condemnations against those it considers its enemies, including clerics.
- **Nature of charges:** Accused of alleged violence against Martha Candelaria Rivas Hernández, later imprisoned for false testimony.

The case of Father Manuel Lavador García sheds light on a distressing pattern of persecution and suppression targeting religious figures in Nicaragua under the regime of President Daniel Ortega. Father García, serving as the Pastor of the Jesús de Nazareno church in the municipality of Nandaime within the Diocese of Granada, became a prominent victim of this unsettling trend. His imprisonment marked a significant turning point, as he was the first priest to be detained by the Ortega regime, casting a frightening shadow over the religious community.

The events leading to Father García's arrest unfolded within the context of escalating government-led persecution against religious figures critical of the regime. His apprehension took place on June 1, 2021, under circumstances that raise concerns about the protection of religious freedom and dissenting voices within the country.

Father García was subjected to a legal process that led to his sentencing. He was handed a prison term of two years based on allegations of physical and psychological harm inflicted upon Martha Candelaria Rivas. However, it is important to note that Rivas herself was later accused of providing false testimony.

Sadiel Eugarrios

Nicaragua

- **Gender:** Male
- **Current location:** Miami, Florida
- **Perpetrator:** Nicaragua
- **Religion or Belief:** Christian Catholic
- **Sentence:** 10 years imprisonment
- **Current Status:** Exiled
- **Religious Leader:** Yes
- **Reason for persecution:** Criticizing Religious Freedom Conditions Human Rights Work for Religious Communities Religious Activity Religious Figure & Religious Leadership Role.
- **Nature of charges:** Spreading Propaganda & False or Misleading Ideas, Information, or Materials Subversion

Sadiel Eugarrios was imprisoned in relation to criticism of religious freedom conditions. On August 4, 2022, police prevented several people, including Eugarrios, a priest, from leaving the residence of Bishop Rolando Álvarez as the bishop was on his way to perform mass at a local cathedral. Álvarez had criticized the government's recent closure of several Catholic radio stations and its human rights record. Alvarez, Eugarrios, and the other individuals in the residence remained under de facto house arrest as authorities investigated them for "organizing violent groups" and encouraging them "to carry out acts of hate against the population."

On August 19, 2022, police detained Eugarrios and sent him to the Evaristo Vásquez Sánchez Police Complex. On October 4, 2022, it was revealed that Eugarrios was charged with "conspiracy to undermine national integrity" and "propagation of false news." On January 26, 2023, Eugarrios was reportedly found guilty. Prosecutors reportedly requested 10 years in prison. On February 3, 2023, a judge from the Second Criminal District Court of Trials of Managua sentenced Eugarrios to 10 years in prison.

On February 9, 2023, Eugarrios was released from prison and exiled to the United States. His Nicaraguan nationality was revoked in February 2023.

Alain Toledano

Cuba

Alain Toledano Valiente has been targeted by the Cuban government for over 20 years because of his leadership in the Apostolic Movement, a charismatic Protestant Christian network which the government has refused to register. On 25 June, Cuban State Security gave him a 30-day deadline to leave the country or face the possibility of long-term imprisonment. Pastor Toledano Valiente and his wife, Marilín Alayo Correa, are the leaders of one of the largest churches in terms of attendees in the eastern city of Santiago de Cuba. Over the past 20 years, the church building has been demolished twice by the government and both the pastor and his wife have been subjected to short term arbitrary detention numerous times. In recent years, Pastor Toledano Valiente has been summoned repeatedly by the police and State Security, interrogated and threatened with imprisonment. His daughters have been the targets of bullying and violence at school, orchestrated by school officials with the backing of State Security.

In October 2021, Cuban officials informed Pastor Toledano Valiente, that a criminal case against him had been prepared, meaning he could be arrested and imprisoned at any time. He has been under an intermittent travel ban over the past four years. In July 2019 he was blocked from boarding a flight to attend the United States Ministerial on International Religious Freedom, and was told he was banned from leaving Cuba due to national security concerns. In June 2022, he was stopped again from traveling to the US, this time to attend the Summit of the Americas where he was meant to participate in side events on freedom of religion or belief. Shortly thereafter, he was informed that the travel ban would be lifted on the condition that he leave the country within 30 days.

The pastor and his family received support from US-based Organization Outreach Aid to the Americas (OAA), which worked with US Ambassador-at-Large for International Religious Freedom Rashad Hussain, and the State Department's Bureau of Consular Affairs, to obtain emergency parole for the pastor, allowing him safe entry into the country. Two of the pastor's adult daughters and their children remain in Cuba.

- **Gender:** Male
- **Current location:** Miami, Florida
- **Perpetrator:** Cuba
- **Religion or Belief:** Christian – Protestant
- **Current Status:** Exiled
- **Religious Leader:** Yes
- **Reason for persecution:** Criticizing Religious Freedom Conditions Human Rights Work for Religious Communities Religious Activity Religious Figure & Religious Leadership Role.

Mario Felix Lleonart Barroso

Cuba

Mario Felix Lleonart was born in 1975 to a devout baptist family. Since the age of 12, he felt called to serve in ministry.

February 23, 2011. Pastor Mario was in Havana participating in a retreat, he was detained around noon and was held for 26 hours in the Police State at Santiago de Las Vegas, close to the Havana airport. He was not charged and released on February 24.

October 14-18, 2011. Pastor Lleonart was placed under house arrest, so he is unable to attend the funeral of Laura Pollan, the leader of the Ladies in White.

Marzo, 27, 2012. At 9 pm, while Pastor Lleonart and his wife were visiting a fellow pastor (Misael D. Rodriguez) in Reparto Alamar, Havana, state security showed up at the house of Pastor Rodriguez to inform Pastor Lleonart and his wife would be arrested if they attended Pope Benedict's Mass the next day. They were ordered to remain under house arrest at Pastor Rodriguez's home. Once the Mass was over, security agents showed up at Pastor Rodriguez' home and told Pastor Lleonart he could leave the house.

January 25, 2014. He is arrested at 12:30 in front of his wife and daughters. State security did not present any motives for his arrest.

In 2016, a few hours before President Obama's visit to Cuba, Pastor was arrested.

In 2016, after years of being harassed, detained, and arrested multiple times because of his faith activities, his congregation, parents, as well as the U.S. Embassy in Havana, suggested Pastor Lleonart and his family sought asylum in the United States. Jeffrey De Laurentis, then Chief of Mission at the U.S. Embassy in Havana, issued political refugee visa. They arrived in the United States on August 18, 2016.

- **Gender:** Male
- **Current location:** Waldorf, Maryland
- **Perpetrator:** Cuba
- **Religion or Belief:** Christian – Protestant
- **Current Status:** Exiled
- **Religious Leader:** Yes
- **Reason for persecution:** Criticizing Religious Freedom Conditions Human Rights Work for Religious Communities Religious Activity Religious Figure & Religious Leadership Role.

Luis Enrique Rojas

Venezuela

Mons. Luis Enrique Rojas Ruiz was born on August 31, 1968 in Merida. On July 12, 2023, the Vatican Press Office reported that Pope Francis has appointed Bishop Luis Enrique Rojas Ruiz, until now Auxiliary Bishop of Merida, as the new Bishop of Punto Fijo in Venezuela.

Monsignor Luis Enrique Rojas, was detained by Venezuelan military forces when he was trying to reach Tovar, the town most affected by the rains on August 29, 2021. Rojas was carrying a shipment of aid sent by Cardinal Baltazar Porras from Caracas.

A day later, the Venezuelan Episcopal Conference (CEV) issued a statement condemning this attitude of the military.
"We regret and reproach the attitude of some civil authorities, as well as the Bolivarian National Guard (GNB), who, far from cooperating disinterestedly, have not only impeded the access of much of the aid sent from various parts of the country, but have had an attitude of disregard and offense towards members of the Church and other institutions," they stated this Monday, August 30.

President Nicolás Maduro accused and threatened the Venezuelan bishops of leading a campaign against the Bolivarian National Armed Forces (Fanb), due to the denunciations made against the obstacles imposed by the military to the delivery of humanitarian aid by the Catholic Church in Mérida.

- **Gender:** Male
- **Current location:** Punto Fijo, Venezuela
- **Perpetrator:** Venezuela
- **Religion or Belief:** Christian – Catholic
- **Religious Leader:** Yes
- **Reason for persecution:** Humanitarian Aid Work for Religious Communities Religious Activity Religious Figure & Religious Leadership Role.

Jairo Pérez

Venezuela

Parishes of the Metropolitan Church of Caracas denounced that the Bolivarian National Intelligence Service (SEBIN) and the Military Counterintelligence Directorate (DGCIM) detained Jairo Perez, catechist and lay activist working in parish churches.

On July 14, 2021 at five o'clock in the afternoon, in La Vega, southwest of Caracas. "The Sebin entered the house of Jairo Perez, about 50 years old. A family father, merchant and social fighter who lives in the Los Mangos sector," said Father Alfredo Infante, parish priest of San Alberto Hurtado.

The Jesuit described that "they entered Jairo's house with guns. They held him and his team at gunpoint during a recreational activity with children". He explained that Jairo, among other community activities, carries out every Wednesday, a cinema forum for children, young people and adults. "At the end, they discuss values," he said.

Alfredo Infante considers that this fact "is an intimidation, a blackmail, towards all the alternative and community works". The truth is that Jairo Perez, who is also a Caritas activist and lives in the limits of the parishes of San Alberto Hurtado (upper part of La Vega) and Santo Cristo (lower part), was missing for 10 days, until the day of his release on July 24.

The social leader of the parish of La Vega, Jairo Perez, was released from prison on the night of July 24, 2021

- **Gender:** Male
- **Current location:** Caracas, Venezuela
- **Perpetrator:** Venezuela
- **Religion or Belief:** Christian - Catholic
- **Reason for persecution:** Religious Communities Religious Activity Religious Figure

Castor Álvarez

Cuba

- **Gender:** Male
- **Current location:** Camagüey, Cuba.
- **Perpetrator:** Cuba
- **Religion or Belief:** Christian – Catholic
- **Reason for persecution:** Criticizing Religious Freedom Conditions Human Rights Work for Religious Communities Religious Activity Religious Figure & Religious Leadership Role.

The priest of the Archdiocese of Camagüey Castor José Álvarez Devesa is fifty years old and lives in the city of Camagüey, Cuba. On the outskirts of the island's third largest city, among the most rural communities in the country, he carries out his welfare and evangelizing work.

On July 11, 2021, during the largest protests in decades against the Castro regime, he was beaten by supporters of the revolution with a baseball bat, received four stitches and was arrested.

Castor Alvarez was held all afternoon and early morning at the Montecarlo police station in Camagüey, accused of public disorder. The priest was detained while defending some young demonstrators.

Father Alvarez was released the following day. The release took place thanks to the efforts of Archbishop Willy Pino, Archbishop of Camagüey.

Enrique Fundora

Cuba

The pastor aEnrique de Jesús Fundora Pérez, was born in the province of Camagüey in 1995.

In 2017, 26-year-old Pastor Enrique de Jesús Fundora and his wife established a ministry they named God Shakes Cuba and the Nations a part of the Apostolic and Prophetic Movement. This immediately made them a target of the government and cost Pastor Fundora his job as a chef in a private restaurant.

In July 2021 Pastor Fundora began to open 'houses of prayer' where he met with the relatives of people imprisoned because of their involvement in the 11 July protests, to pray for them and comfort them. In January 2022 Fundora was summoned by State Security, Cuba's intelligence agency. He was interrogated and accused of holding conspiratorial meetings and of buying water and distributing it to those who had participated in the protests.

In an ambush on 1 March 2022, Pastor Fundora was captured by State Security agents. After a prolonged interrogation, he was given eight days to leave the island or face a 30-year prison sentence for the crimes of rebellion, public disorder, and for being a counterrevolutionary and terrorist.

Within a matter of days, friends and family managed to buy a flight to Serbia with a stopover in Switzerland, for him. Pastor Fundora fled Cuba on his own in March 2022 and received asylum in Switzerland, where a local Latino Christian community welcomed him and provided support to purchase plane tickets for his wife and daughter, who joined him in Switzerland a few weeks later.

Switzerland is now the new home of this young couple, who continue to work for freedom of religion or belief in Cuba even from beyond its borders.

- **Gender:** Male
- **Current location:** Switzerland
- **Perpetrator:** Cuba
- **Religion or Belief:** Christian – Protestant
- **Reason for persecution:** Criticizing Religious Freedom Conditions Human Rights Work for Religious Communities Religious Activity Religious Figure & Religious Leadership Role.

— 159 —

Jorge Luis Pérez Soto

Cuba

Jorge Luis Pérez Soto was born December 23, 1981. Born in Güines, Mayabeque. He is currently parish priest of San Francisco de Paula, Havana.

Cuban priest Jorge Luis Perez Soto denounced that he was not allowed to enter the University of Havana where Cardinal Benjamino Stella, who was sent by Pope Francis, was giving a speech.
Perez Soto, who hails from the San Francisco de Paula parish in the town of Diez de Octubre, had been invited to the event by the church. However, he was later taken off the list by "other" people.

- **Gender:** Male
- **Current location:** Havana, Cuba
- **Perpetrator:** Cuba
- **Religion or Belief:** Christian – Catholic
- **Reason for persecution:** Criticizing Religious Freedom Conditions Human Rights Work for Religious Communities Religious Activity Religious Figure & Religious Leadership Role.

Rolando Montes de Oca

Cuba

Rolando Gisbert Montes de Oca Valero, was born August 26, 1981 in Camagüey.

In January 2021, the clergyman was one of the Cuban priests who wrote the open letter "I have seen the affliction of my people", a letter that criticizes the corruption and inequality prevailing in Cuba and advocates political changes.

- **Gender:** Male
- **Current location:** Camagüey, Cuba.
- **Perpetrator:** Cuba
- **Religion or Belief:** Christian – Catholic
- **Reason for persecution:** Criticizing Religious Freedom Conditions Human Rights Work for Religious Communities Religious Activity Religious Figure & Religious Leadership Role.

On September 19, 2021 he denounced that his parish house, in Camagüey, had been attacked, when unidentified assailants threw two eggs against one of the walls of the house of God and left a written message with the words "Gusano Asqueroso", which the religious leader described as "an aggression of strong symbolic violence".

On January 15, 2022 priest Rolando Montes de Oca, denounced that the parish house where he resides, in the Archdiocese of Camagüey, was again vandalized with eggs against its front door.

"More eggs against my parish house in Vertientes, again in my absence. This time many more than last time, (they estimate about ten) although now without the note of 'disgusting worm' that they left me on that occasion", denounced the priest.

Notes
Index of acronyms and translations

- ANC- National Constituent Assembly

- CCC – Cuban Council of Churches (Consejo de Iglesias de Cuba)

- CCP – Cuban Communist Party (Partido Comunista de Cuba)

- CDR – Committees for Defence of the Revolution (Comités para la Defensa de la Revolución)

- CDE-Corazones de Esperanza (Venezuela)

- CRS-U.S. Congressional Research Service

- CIMPEC – Interdenominational Fellowship of Ministers and Pastors in Cuba

- (Confraternidad Interdenominacional de Ministros y Pastores en Cuba)

- CONSEJO-Consejo Interreligioso Compuesto

- CUC – Convertible Cuban Pesos

- DJR- Directorate of Justice and Religion (Venezuela)

- ECV-Episcopal Conference of Venezuela

- HRW-Human Rights Watch

- IACHR-Inter-American Commission on Human Rights

- ICCPR – International Covenant on Civil and Political Rights

- ICECSR – International Covenant on Economic, Cultural and Social Rights

- LFOs- Local Faith Organizations

- MOCEV-Evangelical Christian Movement for Venezuela

- NRC-National Religious Council (Venezuela)

- NGOs- Non-Governmental Organizations

- OCHA-U.N. Office for the Coordination of Humanitarian Affairs

- ONCDOFT-National Offioce Against Organized Crime and Terrorism   Financing

- ORA – Office of Religious Affairs

- PSUV-United Socialist Party of Venezuela

- USAID-United States Agency for International Development

- USCIRF-U.S. Commission on International Religious Freedom

- UN-United Nation's

- VAU-Venezuela Affairs Unit

About the Photos in this Book

The images featured in this book have been sourced from the author's personal collection, are in the public domain, or have been included with the subject's consent, where applicable.

www.ingramcontent.com/pod-product-compliance
Lightning Source LLC
Chambersburg PA
CBHW060042030426
42334CB00019B/2448